FOR ORGANS, PIANOS & ELECTRONIC KEYBOARDS

E-Z PLAY® TODAY

61

ADELE 30

T0088838

ISBN 978-1-70516-045-9

E-Z Play® Today Music Notation © 1975 by HAL LEONARD LLC
E-Z PLAY and EASY ELECTRONIC KEYBOARD MUSIC are registered trademarks of HAL LEONARD LLC.

Visit Hal Leonard Online at
www.halleonard.com

Contact us:
Hal Leonard
7777 West Bluemound Road
Milwaukee, WI 53213
Email: info@halleonard.com

In Europe, contact:
Hal Leonard Europe Limited
42 Wigmore Street
Marylebone, London, W1U 2RY
Email: info@halleonardeurope.com

In Australia, contact:
Hal Leonard Australia Pty. Ltd.
4 Lentara Court
Cheltenham, Victoria, 3192 Australia
Email: info@halleonard.com.au

Strangers by Nature

Registration 8
Rhythm: Ballad

Words and Music by Adele Adkins
and Ludwig Göransson

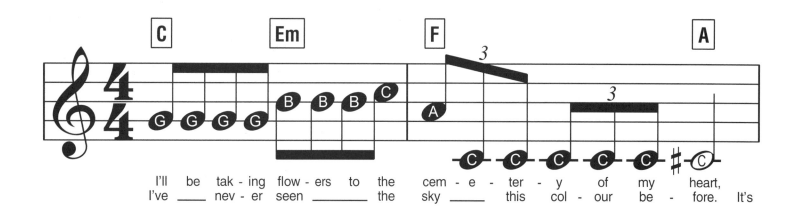

I'll be tak-ing flow-ers to the cem - e - ter - y of my heart,
I've ___ nev-er seen ___ the sky ___ this col-our be - fore. It's

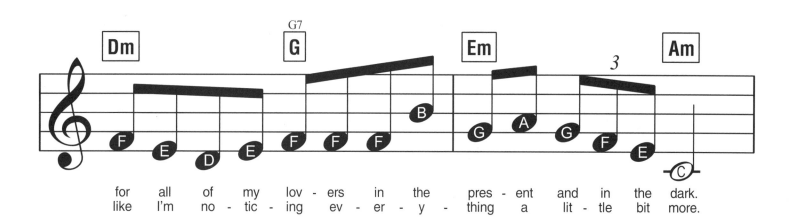

for all of my lov-ers in the pres-ent and in the dark.
like I'm no - tic-ing ev-er-y - thing a lit-tle bit more.

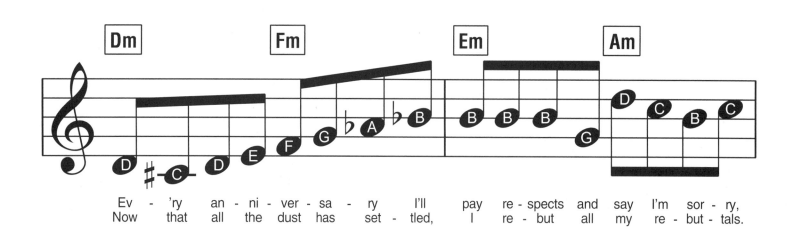

Ev - 'ry an-ni-ver-sa-ry I'll pay re-spects and say I'm sor-ry,
Now that all the dust has set - tled, I re-but all my re-but-tals.

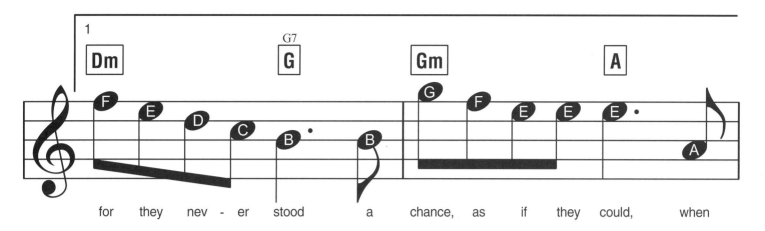

for they nev - er stood a chance, as if they could, when

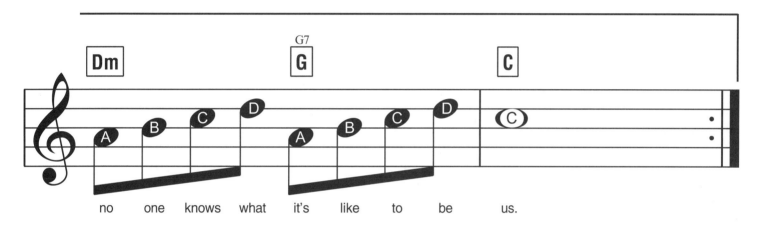

no one knows what it's like to be us.

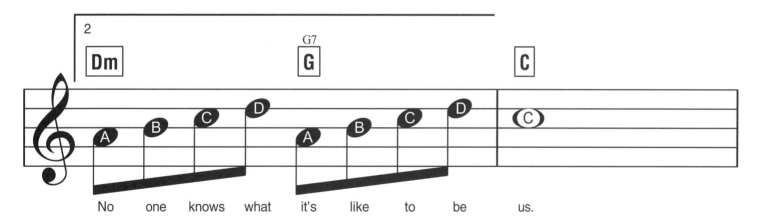

No one knows what it's like to be us.

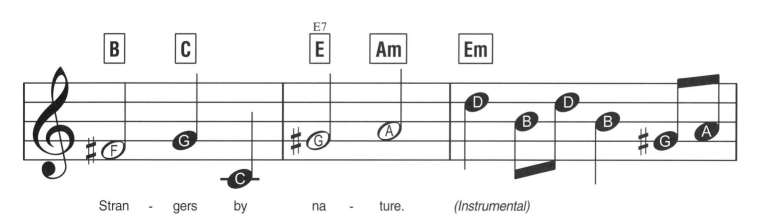

Stran - gers by na - ture. *(Instrumental)*

4

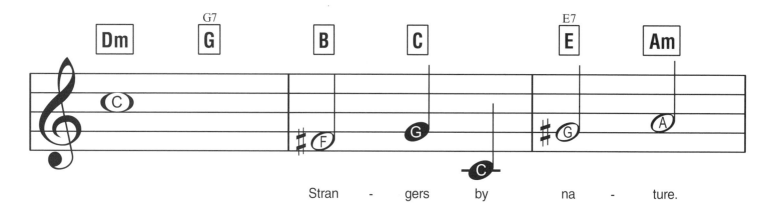

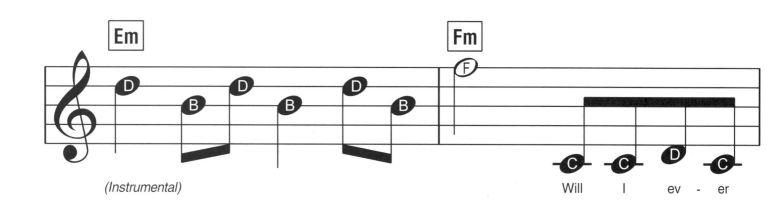

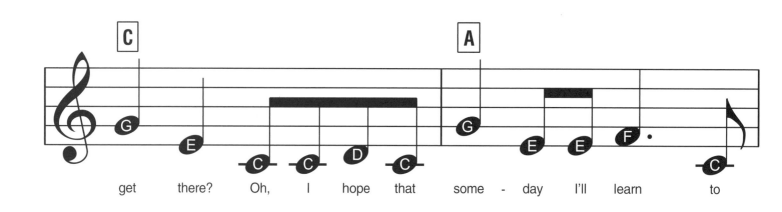

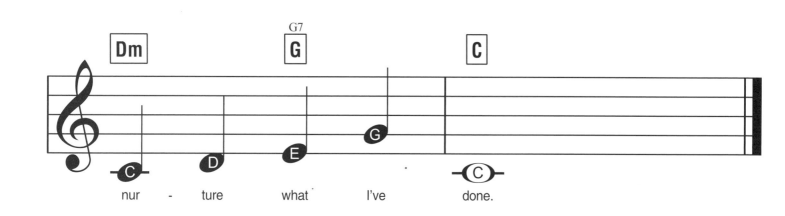

Cry Your Heart Out

Registration 7
Rhythm: Swing or Motown

Words and Music by Adele Adkins
and Greg Kurstin

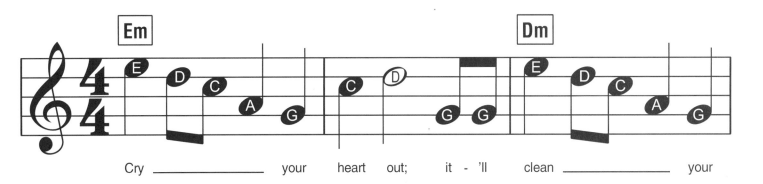

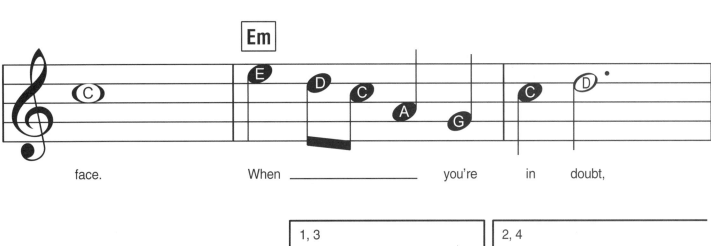

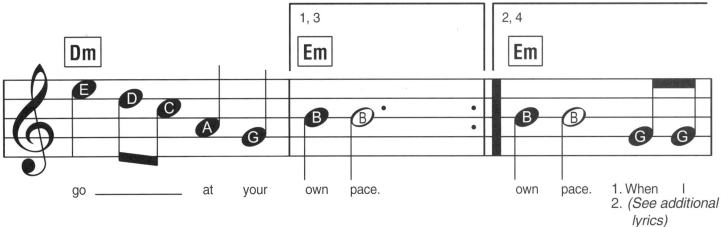

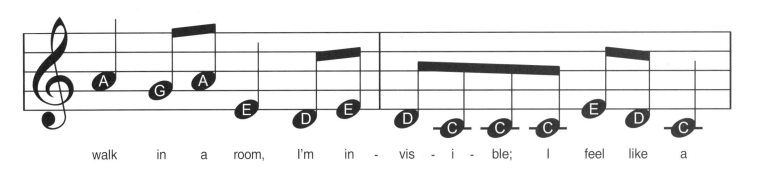

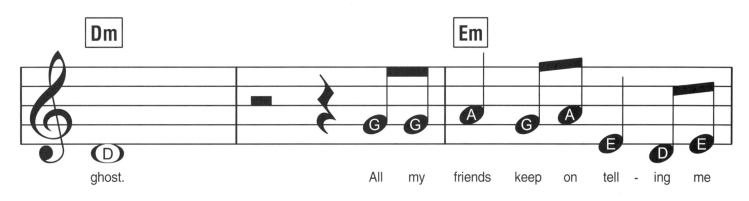

ghost.   All my friends keep on tell - ing me

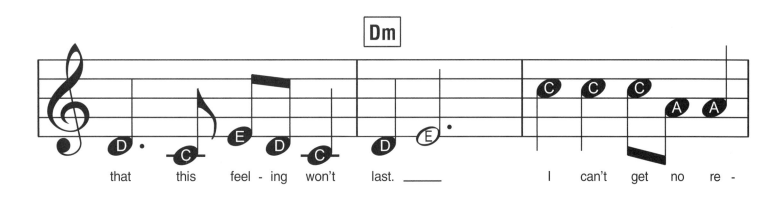

that this feel - ing won't last. _____   I can't get no re -

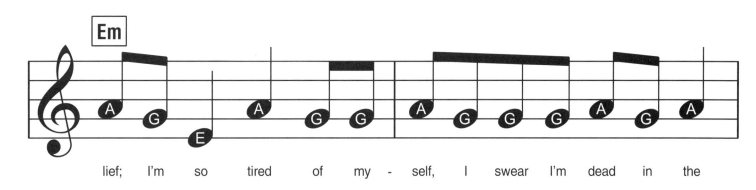

lief; I'm so tired of my - self, I swear I'm dead in the

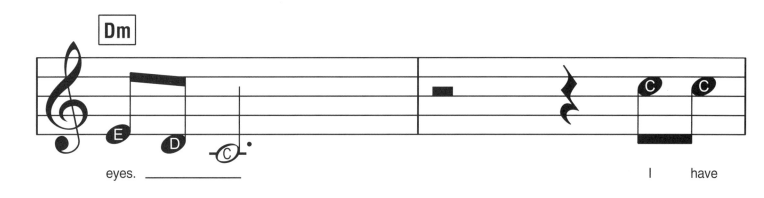

eyes. _____   I have

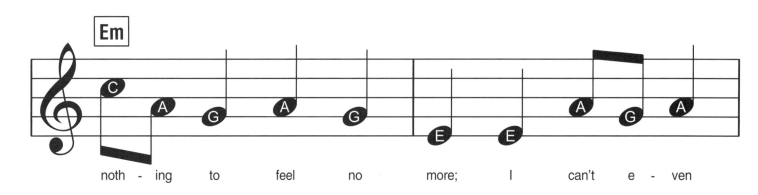

noth - ing to feel no more; I can't e - ven

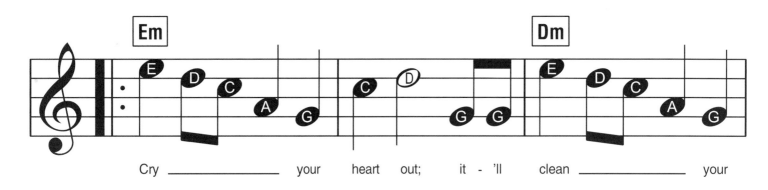

Cry _____ your heart out; it - 'll clean _____ your

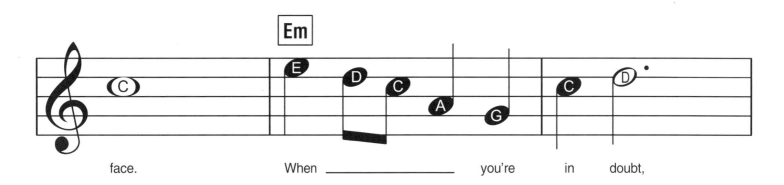

face. When _____ you're in doubt,

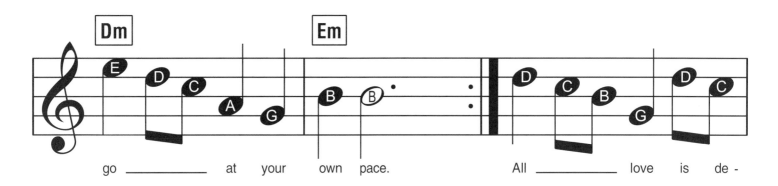

go _____ at your own pace. All _____ love is de -

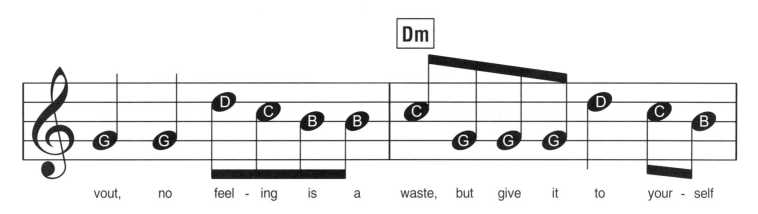

vout, no feel - ing is a waste, but give it to your - self

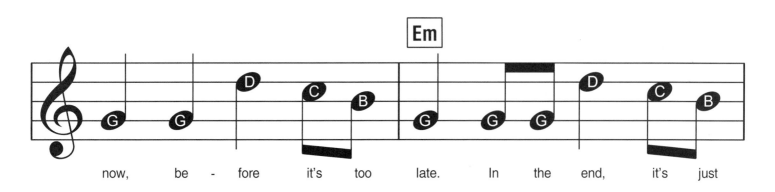

now, be - fore it's too late. In the end, it's just

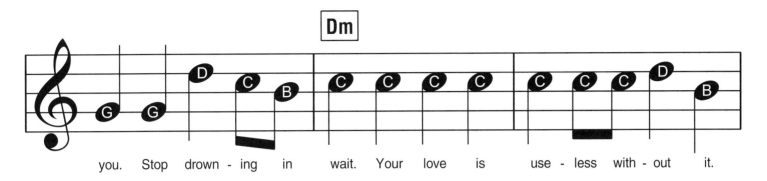

you. Stop drown - ing in wait. Your love is use - less with - out it.

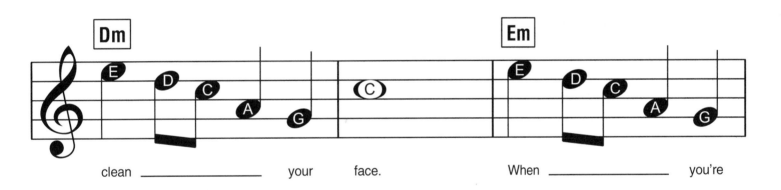

Cry _____ your heart out; it - 'll

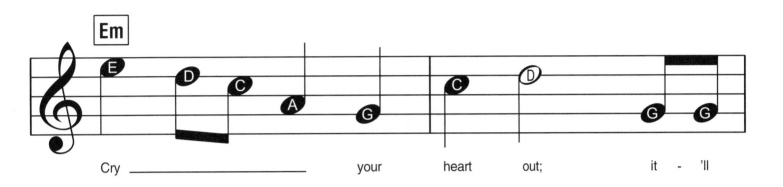

clean _____ your face. When _____ you're

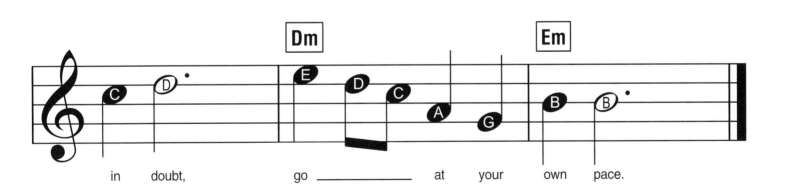

in doubt, go _____ at your own pace.

Additional Lyrics

2. When I wake up, I'm afraid of the idea of facing the day.
   I would rather stay home on my own, drink it all away.
   Please stop calling me; it's exhausting. There's really nothing left to say.
   I created this storm; it's only fair I have to sit in its rain.

Easy on Me

Registration 8
Rhythm: Ballad

Words and Music by Adele Adkins
and Greg Kurstin

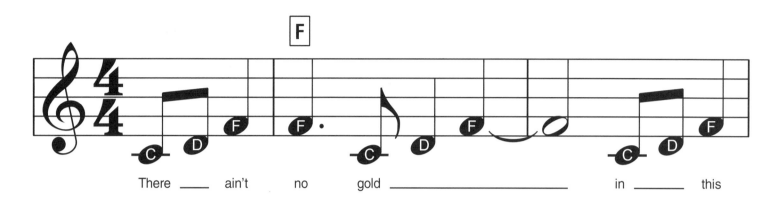

There ____ ain't no gold _____ in ____ this

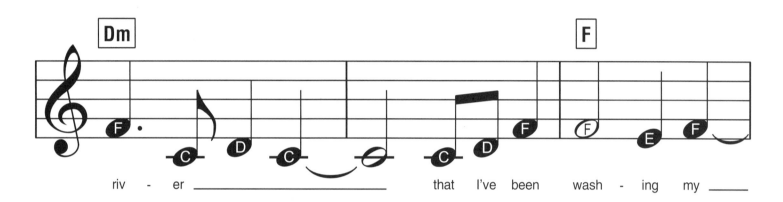

riv - er _____ that I've been wash - ing my ____

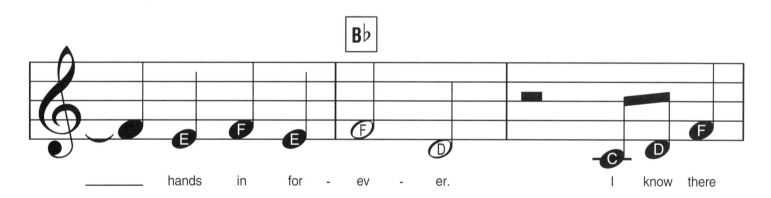

_____ hands in for - ev - er. I know there

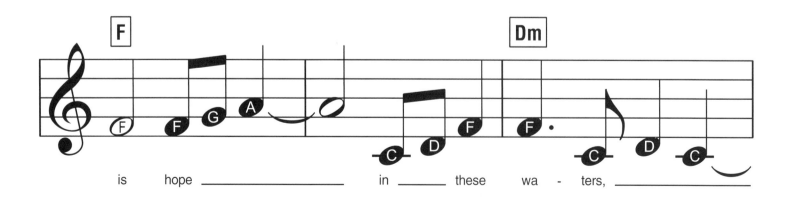

is hope _____ in ____ these wa - ters, _____

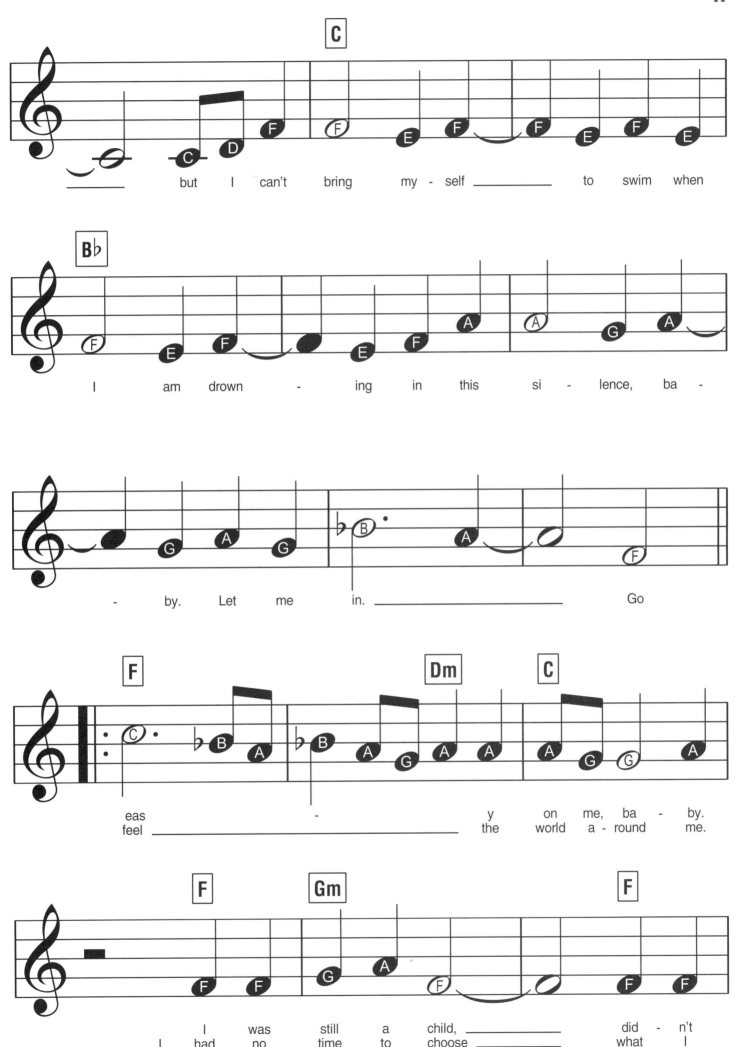

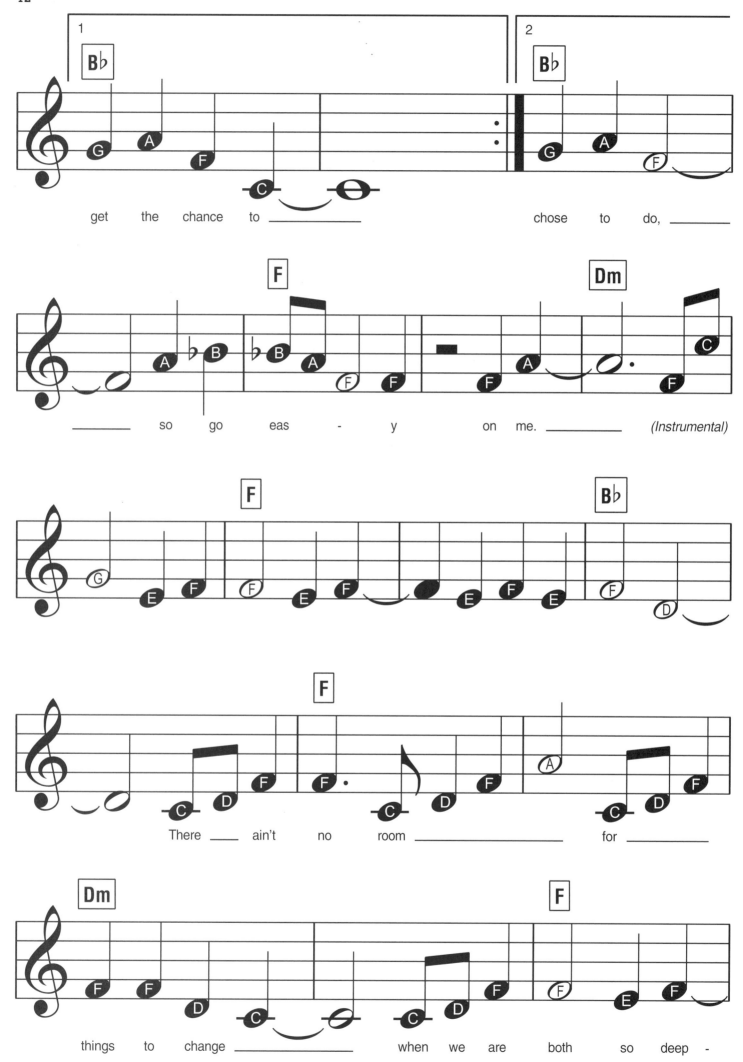

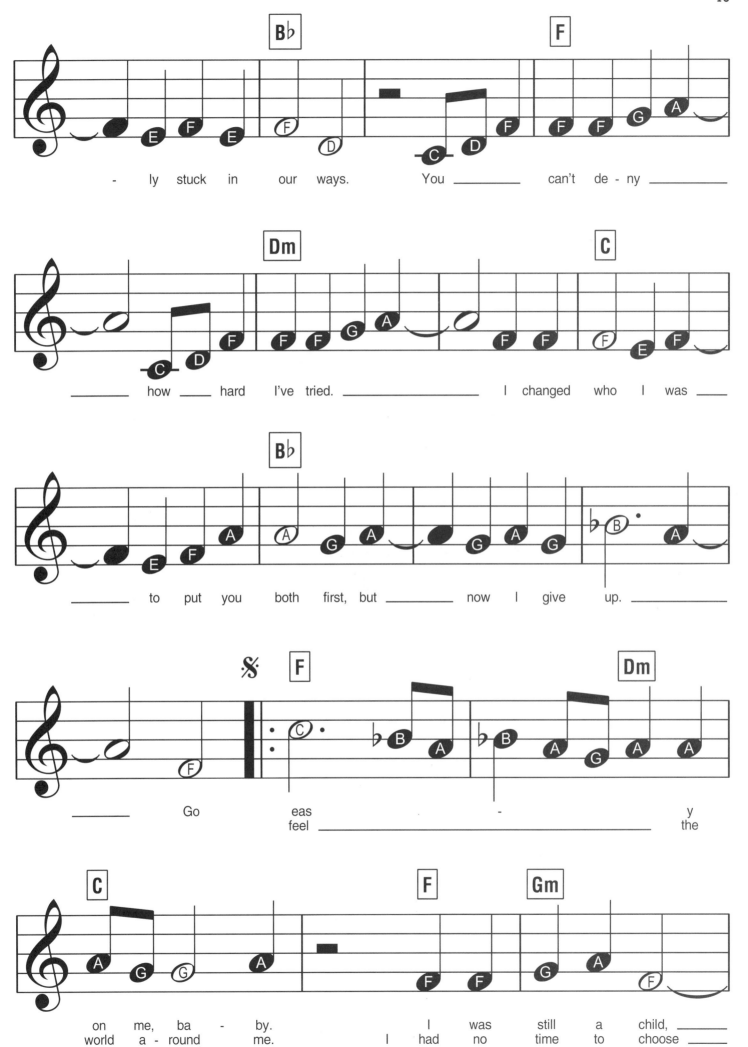

14

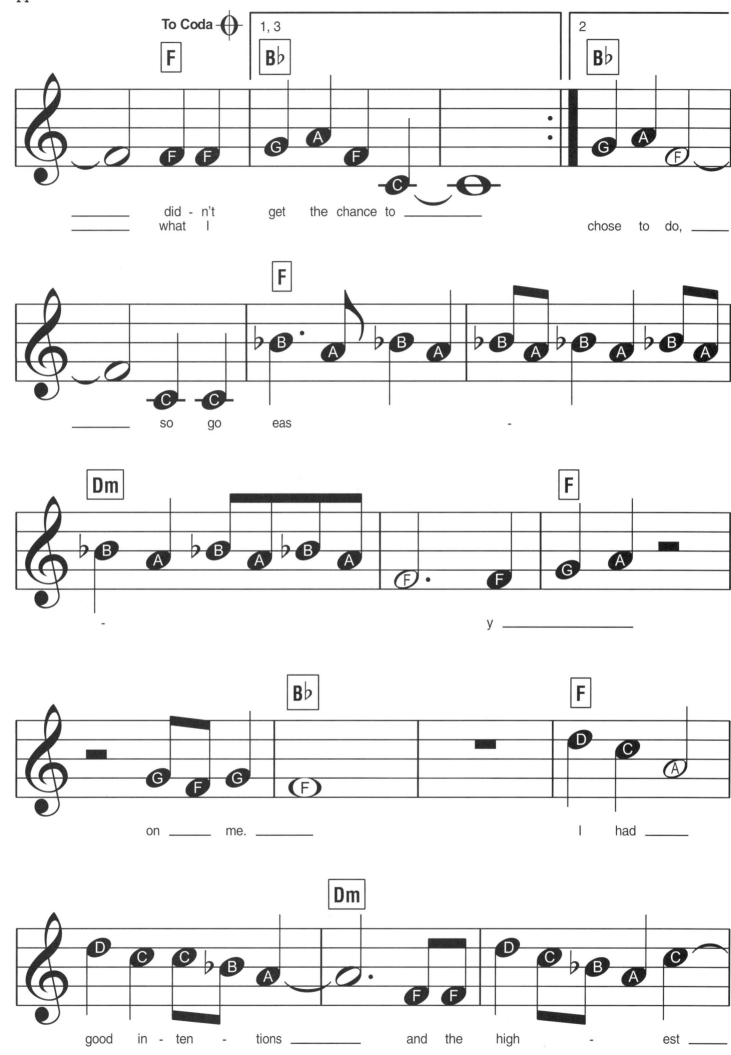

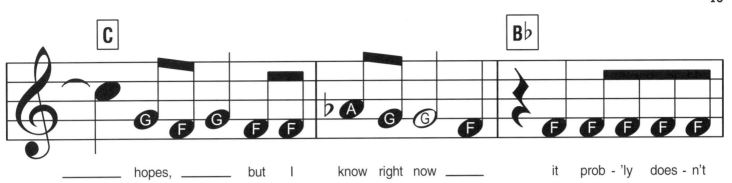

hopes, _____ but I know right now _____ it prob - 'ly does - n't

D.S. al Coda
(Return to 𝄋, play to ⊕
and skip to Coda)

e - ven show. _____ Go

CODA ⊕

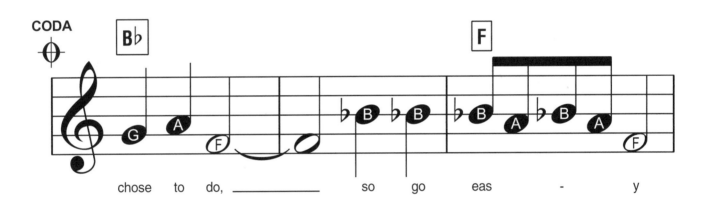

chose to do, _____ so go eas - y

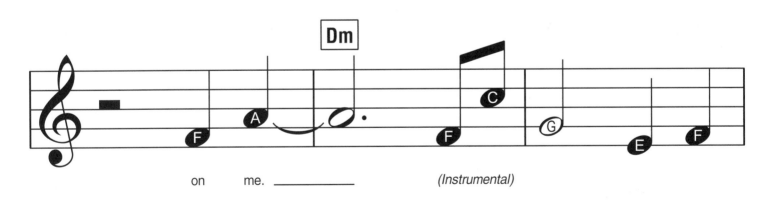

on me. _____ *(Instrumental)*

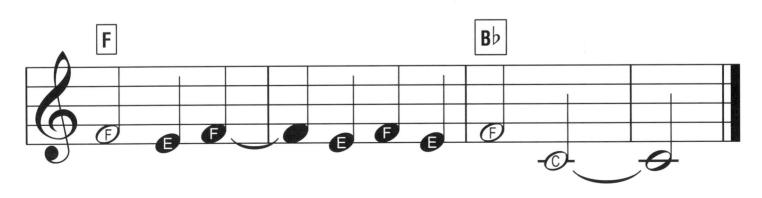

My Little Love

Registration 1
Rhythm: Ballad or Lounge

Words and Music by Adele Adkins
and Greg Kurstin

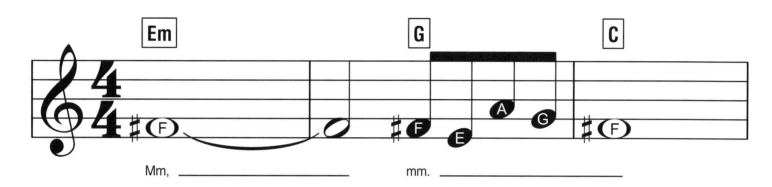

Mm, _____ mm. _____

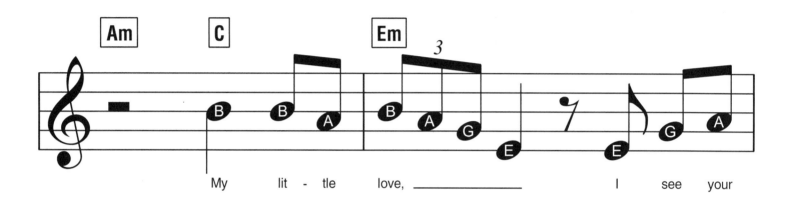

My lit - tle love, _____ I see your

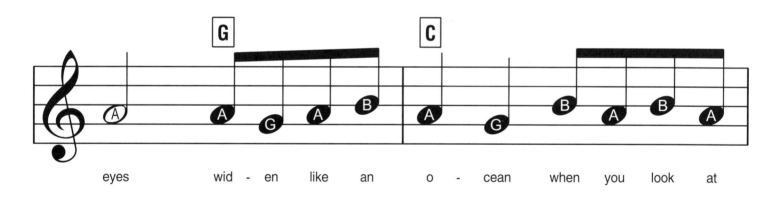

eyes wid - en like an o - cean when you look at

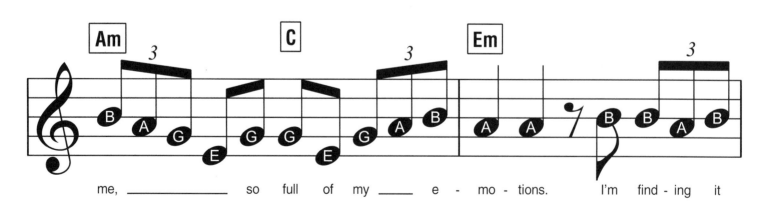

me, _____ so full of my ___ e - mo - tions. I'm find - ing it

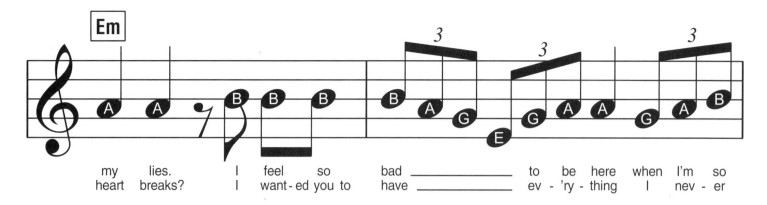

my lies.   I feel so   bad _____ to be here when I'm so
heart breaks? I want-ed you to have _____ ev - 'ry - thing I nev - er

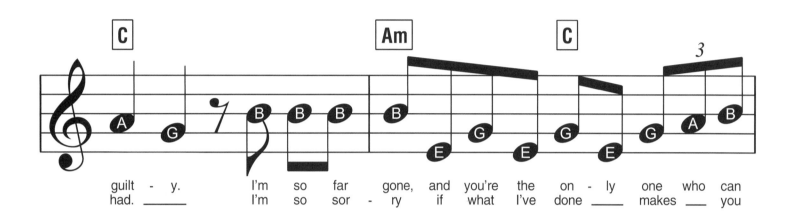

guilt - y.   I'm so far gone, and you're the on - ly one who can
had. ____   I'm so sor - ry if what I've done ___ makes ___ you

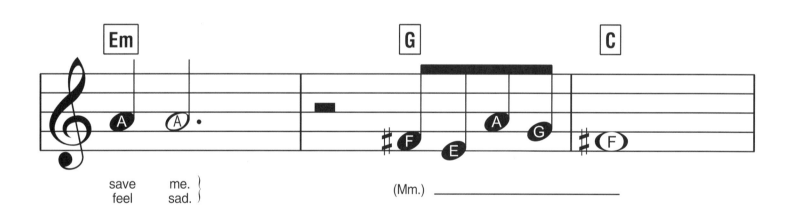

save me. }
feel sad. }   (Mm.) _____

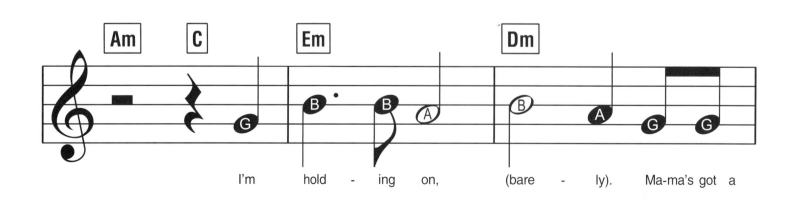

I'm hold - ing on,   (bare - ly). Ma-ma's got a

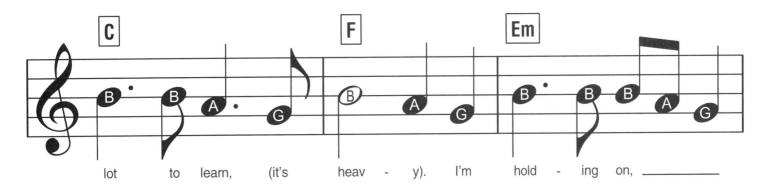

lot to learn, (it's heav - y). I'm hold - ing on, _____

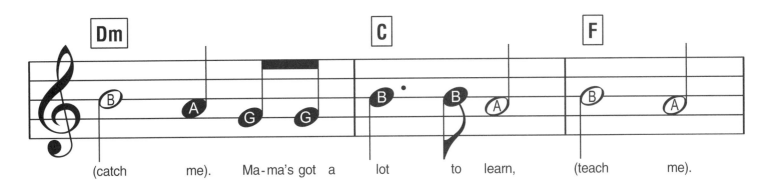

(catch me). Ma - ma's got a lot to learn, (teach me).

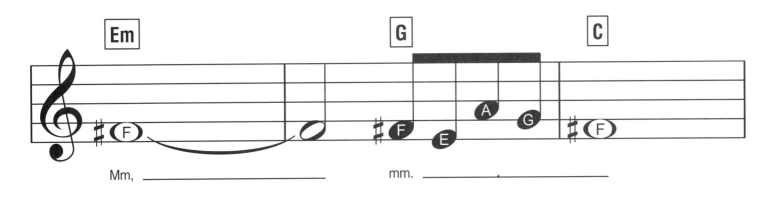

Mm, _____ mm. _____

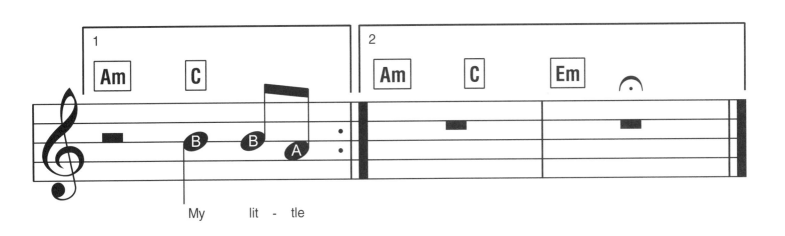

My lit - tle

Oh My God

Registration 7
Rhythm: Funk or Pop

Words and Music by Adele Adkins
and Greg Kurstin

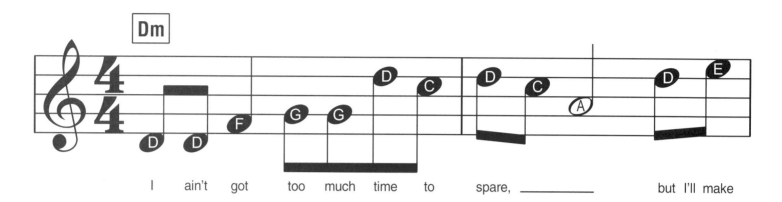

I ain't got too much time to spare, _____ but I'll make

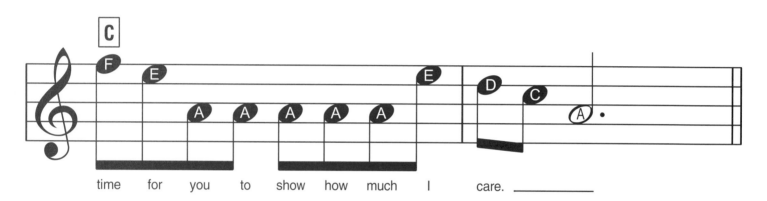

time for you to show how much I care. _____

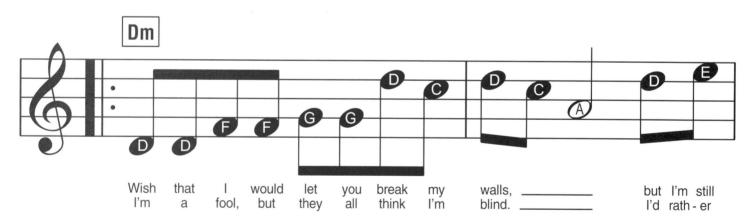

Wish that I would let you break my walls, _____ but I'm still
I'm a fool, but they all think I'm blind. _____ I'd rath - er

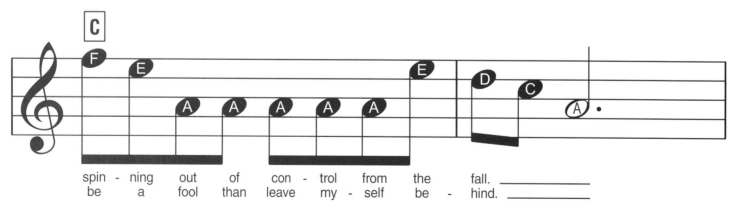

spin - ning out of con - trol from the fall. _____
be a fool than leave my - self be - hind. _____

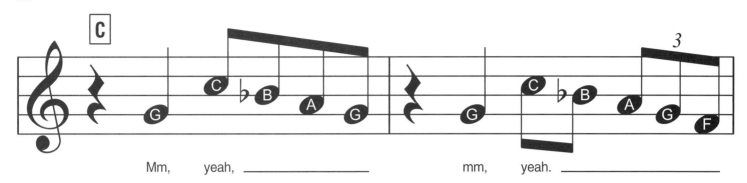

Mm, yeah, _____ mm, yeah. _____

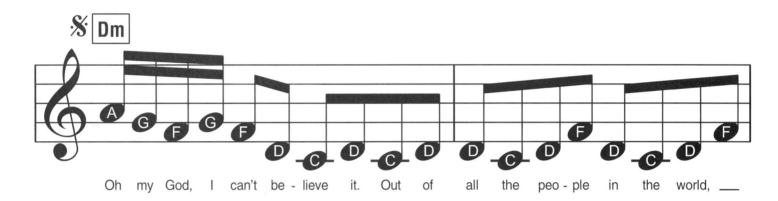

Oh my God, I can't be - lieve it. Out of all the peo - ple in the world, ___

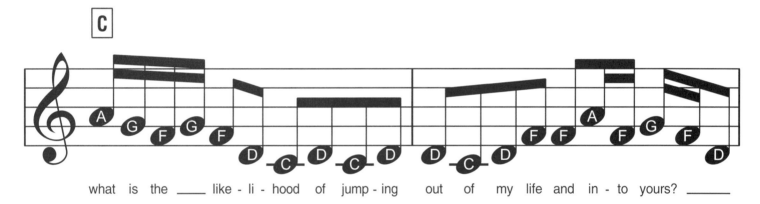

what is the ____ like - li - hood of jump - ing out of my life and in - to yours? _____

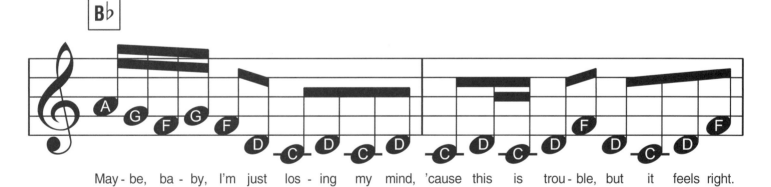

May - be, ba - by, I'm just los - ing my mind, 'cause this is trou - ble, but it feels right.

To Coda ⊕

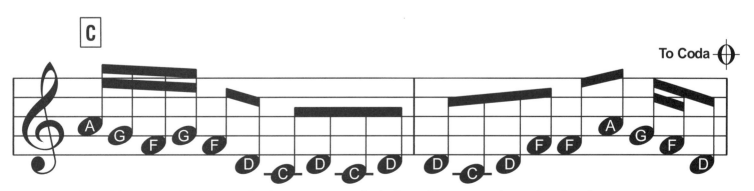

Tee-t'ring on the edge of heav - en and hell, it's a bat - tle that I can - not fight. ___

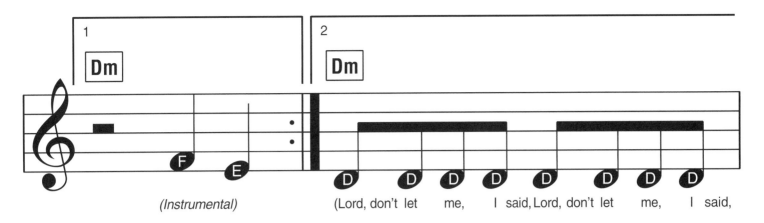

(Instrumental)

(Lord, don't let   me,   I said, Lord, don't let   me,   I said,

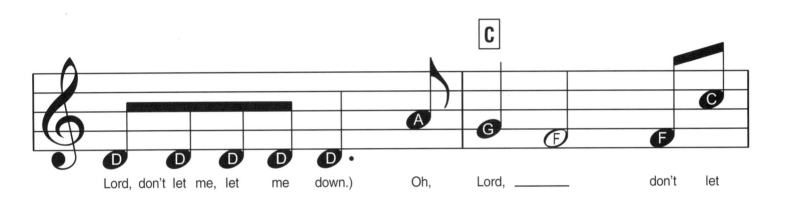

Lord, don't let me, let   me   down.)   Oh,   Lord, _____   don't   let

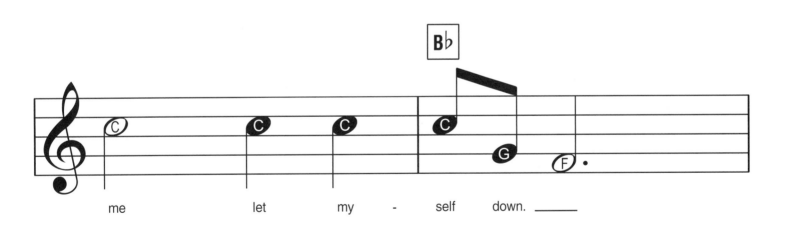

me   let   my - self   down. _____

D.S. al Coda
(Return to 𝄋, play to ⊕
and skip to Coda)

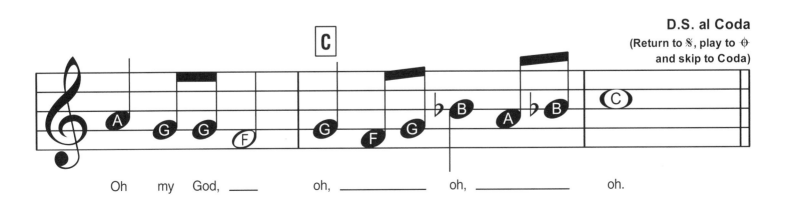

Oh   my   God, ____   oh, _____   oh, _____   oh.

CODA

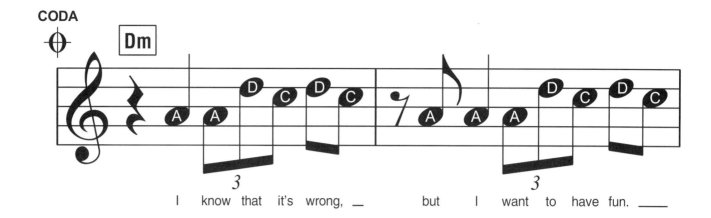

I know that it's wrong, __ but I want to have fun. ____

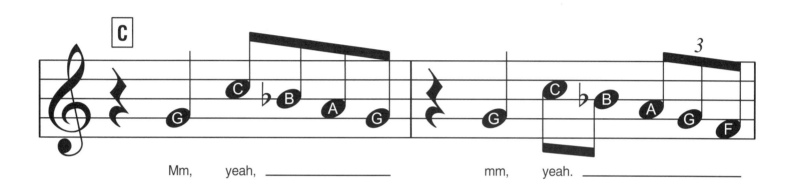

Mm, yeah, _____ mm, yeah. _____

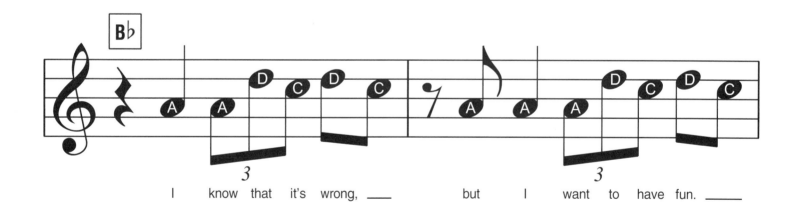

I know that it's wrong, ___ but I want to have fun. _____

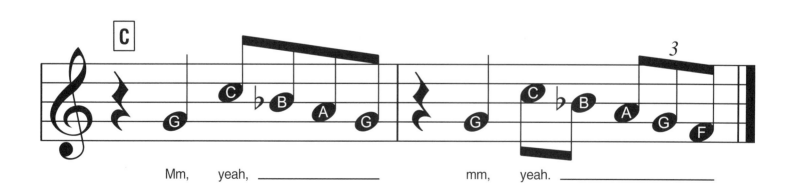

Mm, yeah, _____ mm, yeah. _____

Can I Get It

Registration 4
Rhythm: Pop or Acoustic

Words and Music by Adele Adkins,
Shellback and Max Martin

Pave me a path to fol - low and I'll
Throw me _____ to the wa - ter. I don't
tease me _____ with your con - trol be - cause I

tread an - y dan - ger - ous road. I will
care how _____ deep or shal - low, be - cause and my
long to live un - der your spell, and with -

beg and I'll steal, I will bor - row if I can
heart can _____ pound _____ like thun - der, and your
out your _____ love, _____ I'm hol - low. I won't

make, if I can make your heart my home.
love, _____ and can your love can set me
make it, I won't make it on my

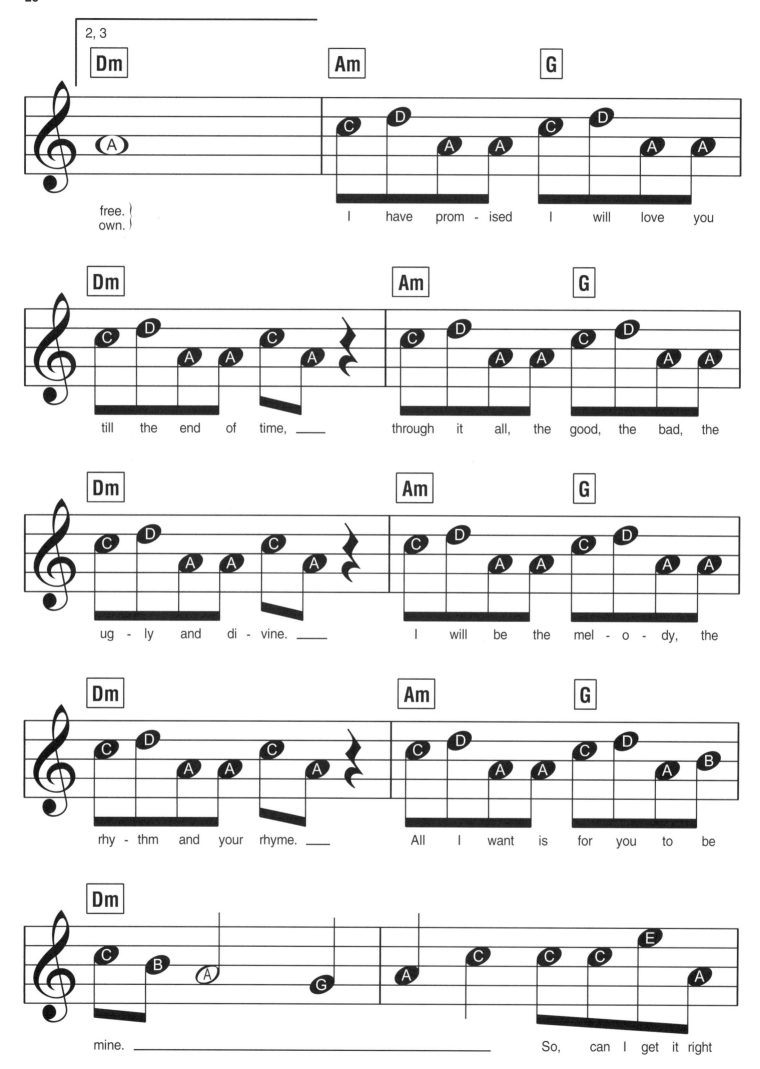

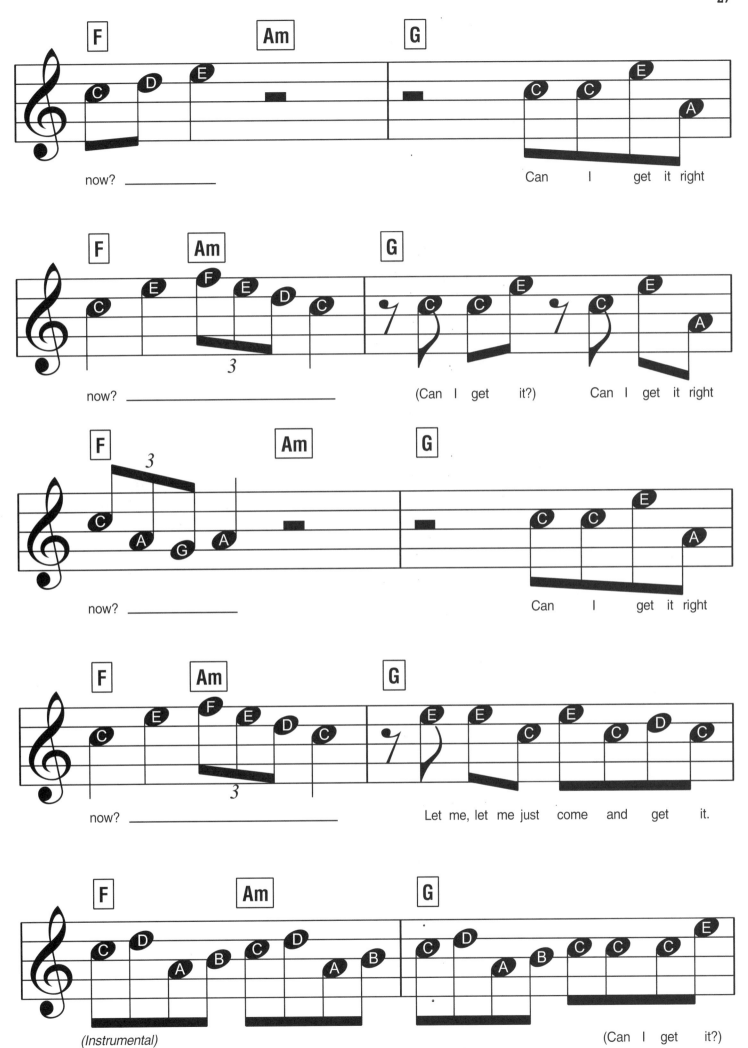

29

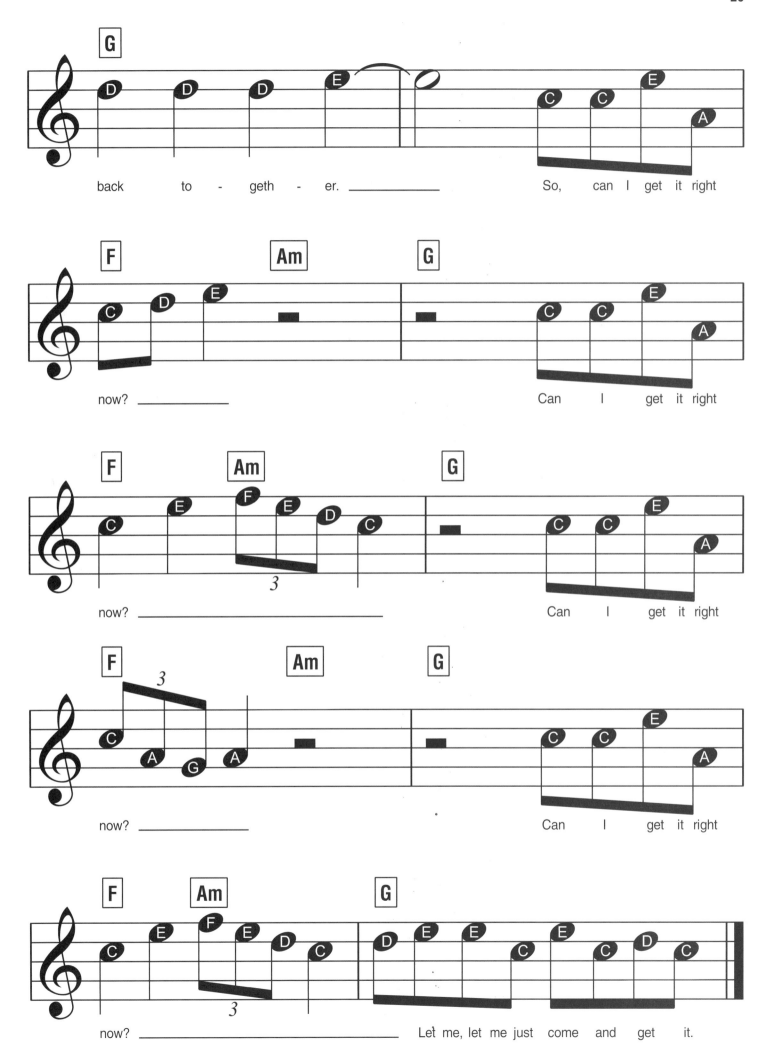

I Drink Wine

Registration 8
Rhythm: Swing Ballad

Words and Music by Adele Adkins
and Greg Kurstin

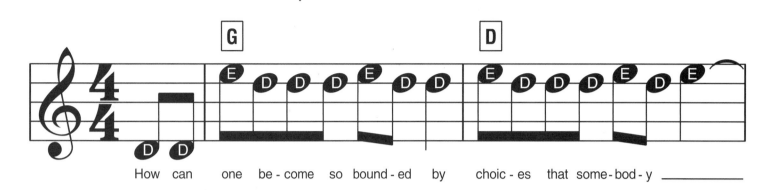

How can one be-come so bound-ed by choic-es that some-bod-y _____

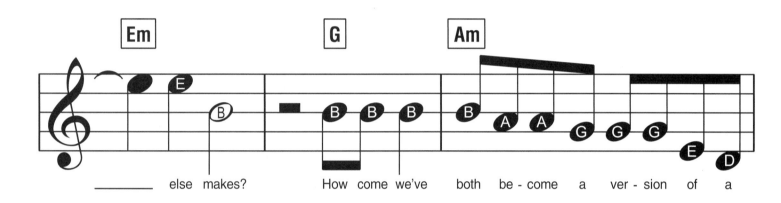

_____ else makes? How come we've both be-come a ver-sion of a

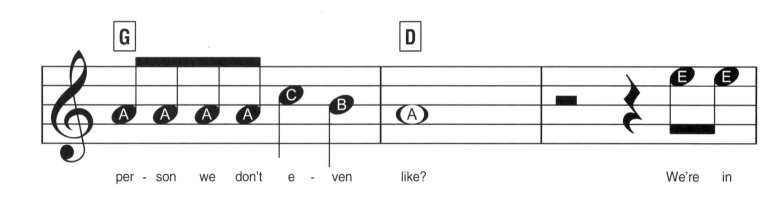

per-son we don't e-ven like? We're in

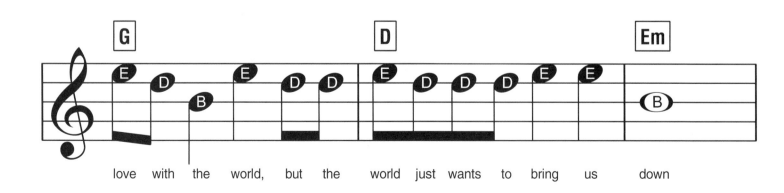

love with the world, but the world just wants to bring us down

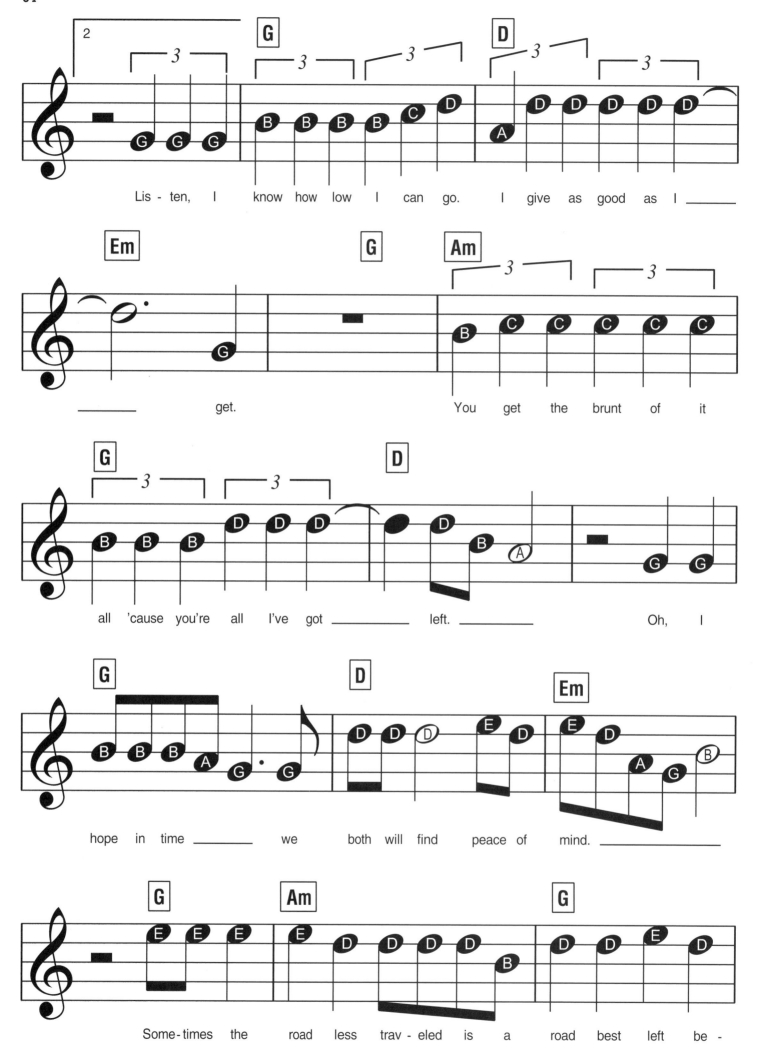

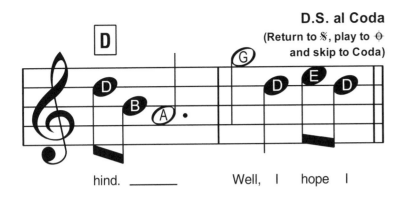

D.S. al Coda
(Return to 𝄋, play to ⊕
and skip to Coda)

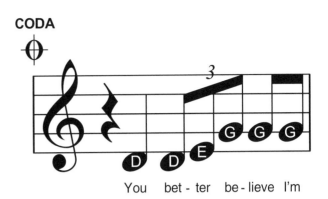

CODA

hind. _____ Well, I hope I

You bet - ter be - lieve I'm

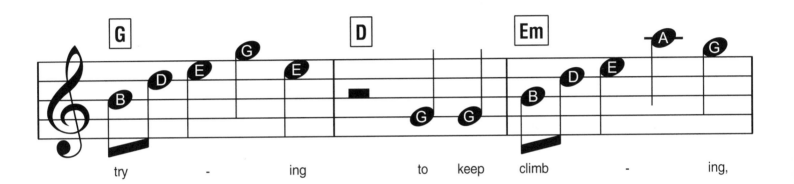

try - ing to keep climb - ing,

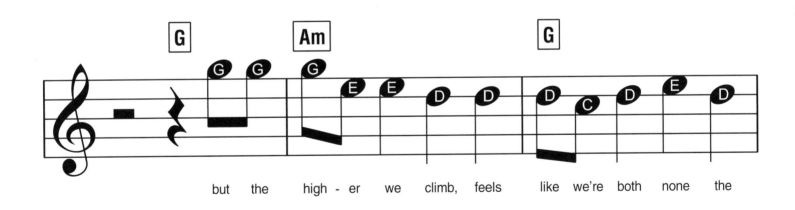

but the high - er we climb, feels like we're both none the

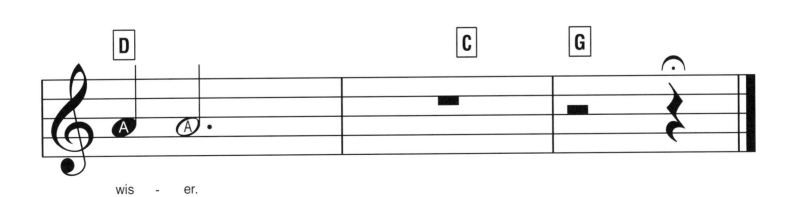

wis - er.

All Night Parking
(Interlude)

Registration 8
Rhythm: Ballad or Lounge

Words and Music by Adele Adkins
and Erroll Garner

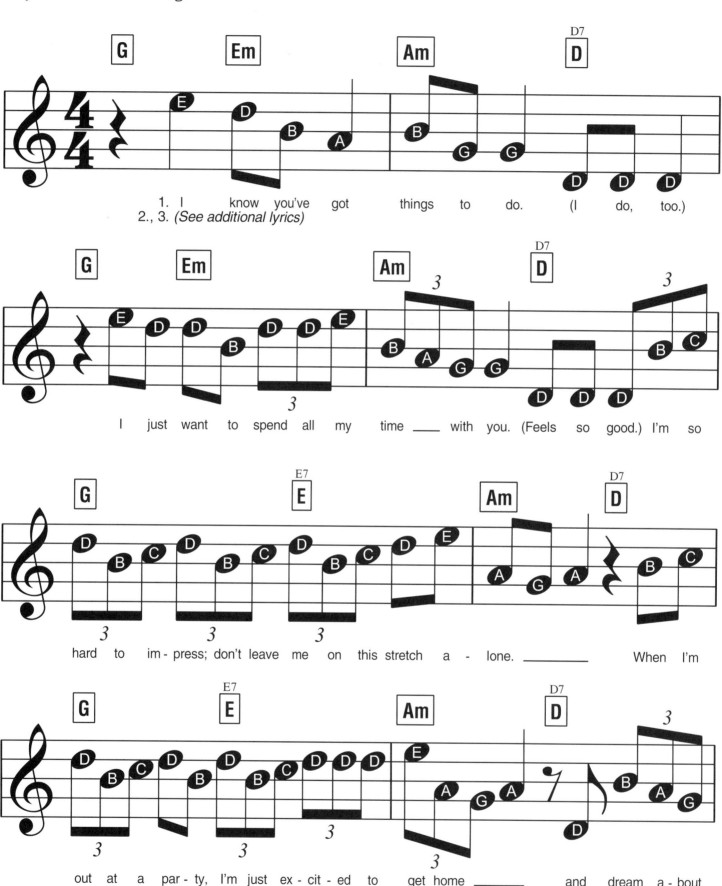

1. I know you've got things to do. (I do, too.)
2., 3. *(See additional lyrics)*

I just want to spend all my time ___ with you. (Feels so good.) I'm so

hard to im - press; don't leave me on this stretch a - lone. ___ When I'm

out at a par - ty, I'm just ex - cit - ed to get home ___ and dream a - bout

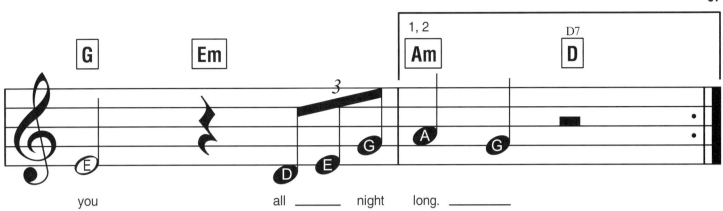

you all _____ night long. _____

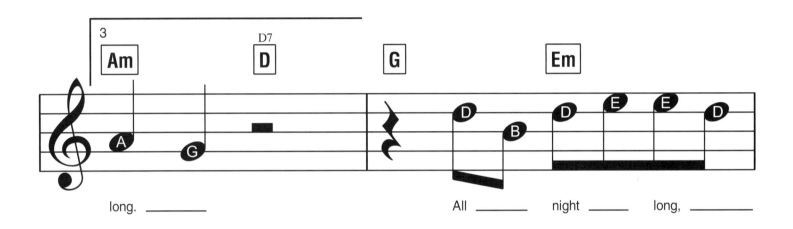

long. _____   All _____ night _____ long, _____

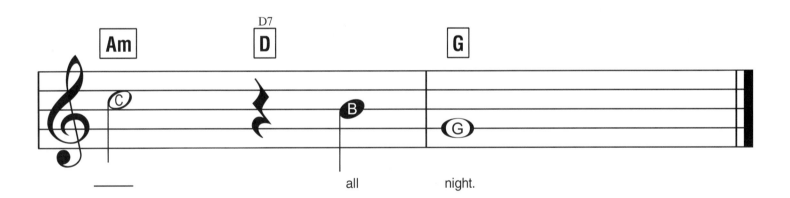

_____   all   night.

Additional Lyrics

2. I don't know how you got through to me. (I'm so cold.)
    It's all happening so easily. (Like, oh my God.)
    It's so hard to digest; usually I'm best alone.
    But every time that you text, I want to get on the next flight home
    And dream next to you all night long.

3. Maybe it's the way you remind me of (where I come from).
    Or how you made me feel beautiful (and then some).
    The sight of you is dramatic; one glimpse and I panic inside.
    I get lost in our hours 'cause you possess powers I can't fight.
    That's why I dream about you all night long.

Woman Like Me

Registration 4
Rhythm: Ballad

Words and Music by Adele Adkins
and Dean Josiah Cover

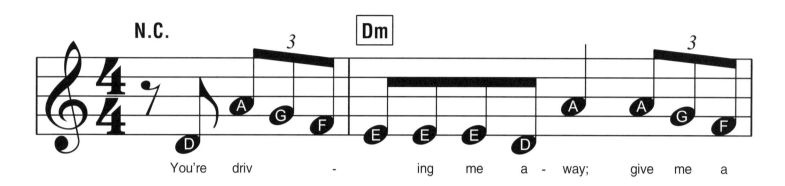

You're driv - ing me a - way; give me a

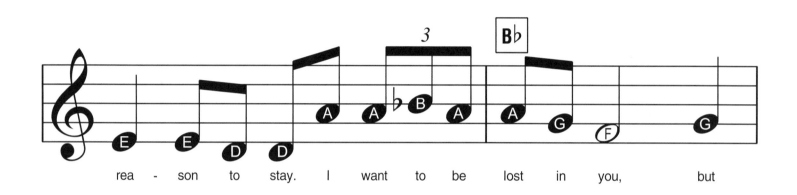

rea - son to stay. I want to be lost in you, but

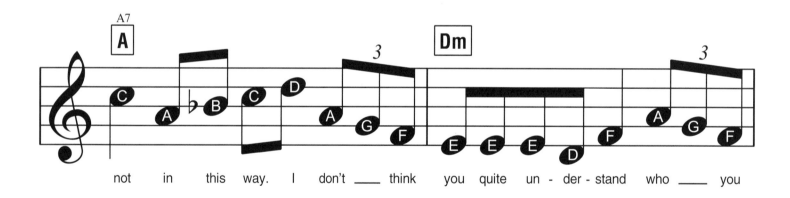

not in this way. I don't ___ think you quite un - der - stand who ___ you

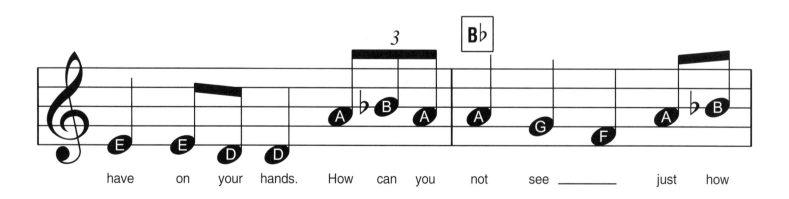

have on your hands. How can you not see _____ just how

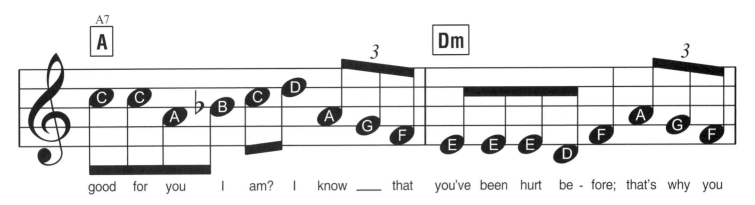

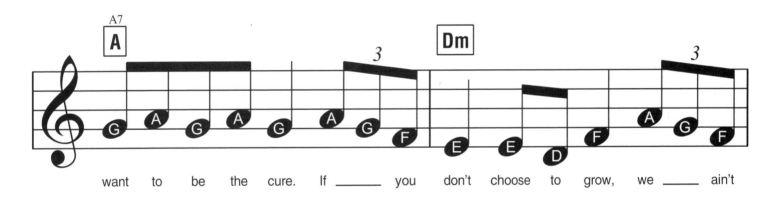

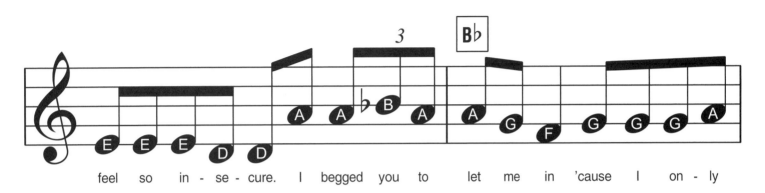

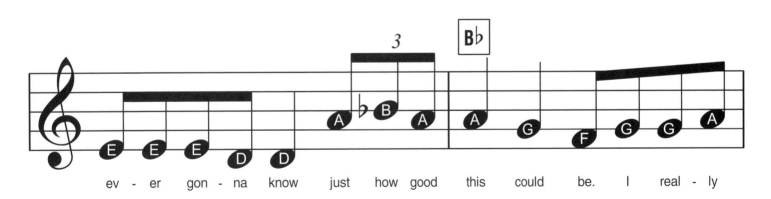

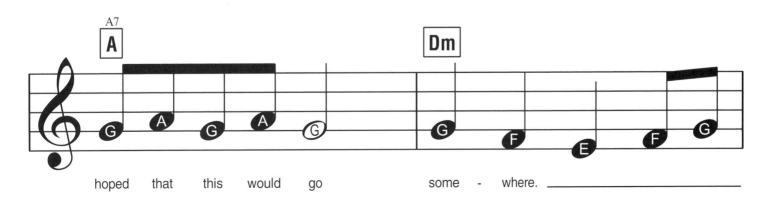

Com - pla - cen -

cy is the worst trait to have. Are you cra - zy? You ain't

ev - er had, ___ ain't ev - er had a wom - an like me. It is

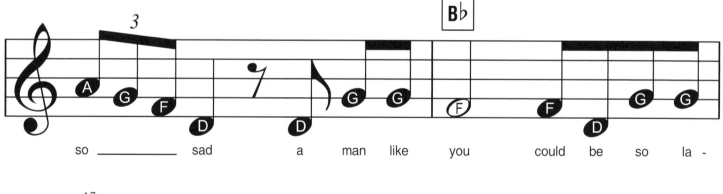

so ___ sad a man like you could be so la -

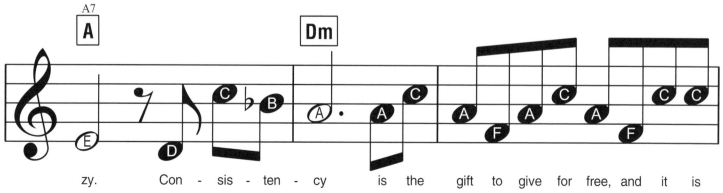

zy. Con - sis - ten - cy is the gift to give for free, and it is

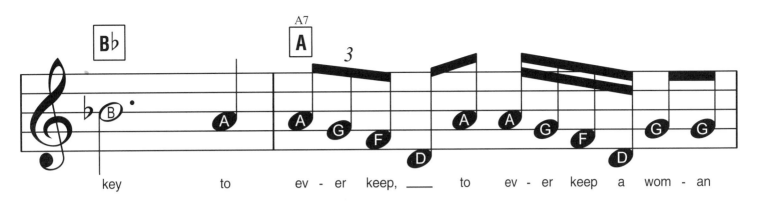

key to ev - er keep, ___ to ev - er keep a wom - an

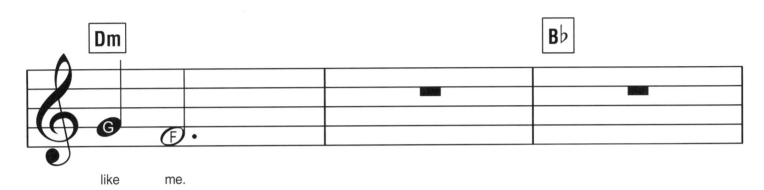

like me.

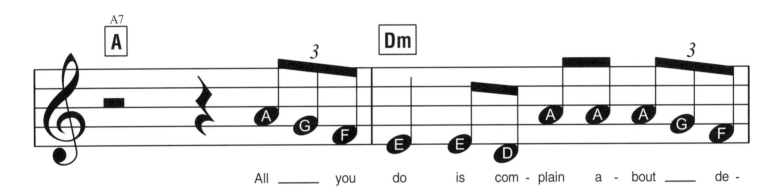

All ___ you do is com - plain a - bout ___ de -

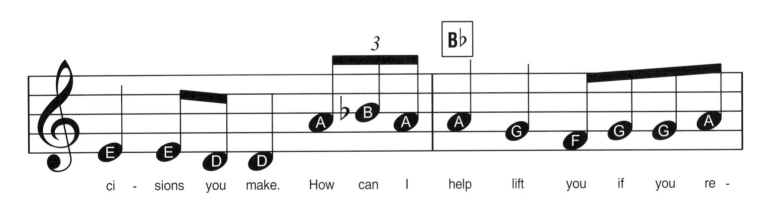

ci - sions you make. How can I help lift you if you re -

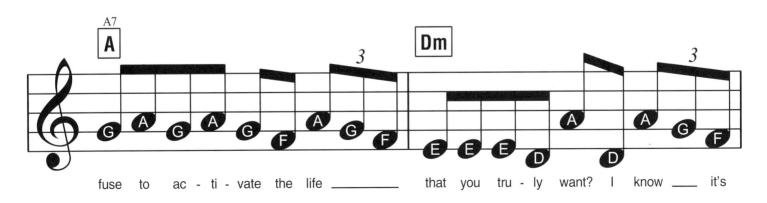

fuse to ac - ti - vate the life ___ that you tru - ly want? I know ___ it's

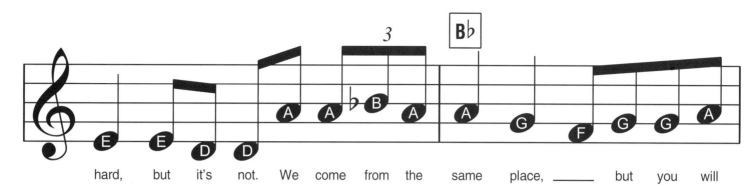

hard, but it's not. We come from the same place, _____ but you will

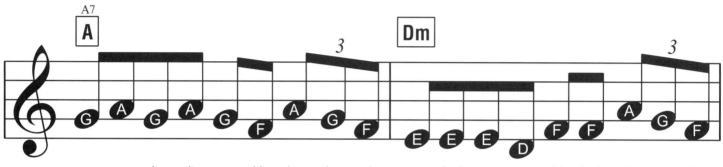

nev - er give it up. It's where they make you feel pow - er - ful; that's why you think

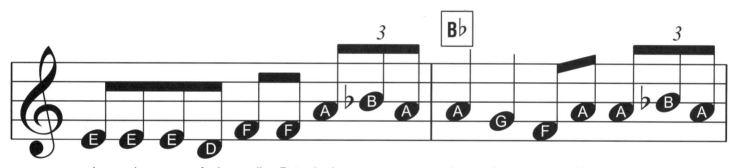

I make you feel small. But that's your pro - jec - tion; _____ it's not my re -

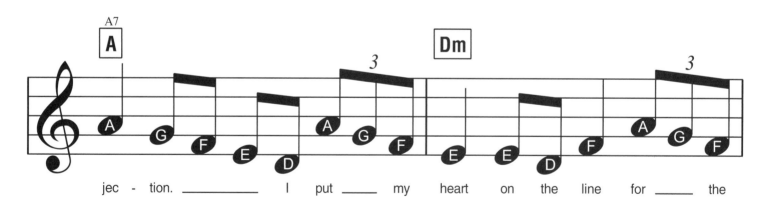

jec - tion. _____ I put _____ my heart on the line for _____ the

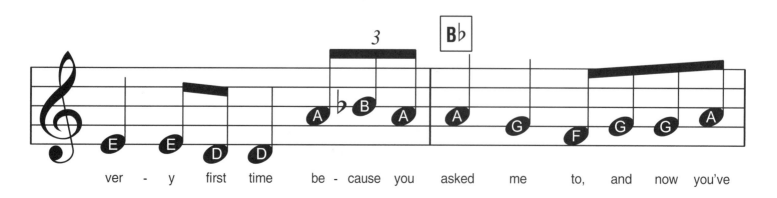

ver - y first time be - cause you asked me to, and now you've

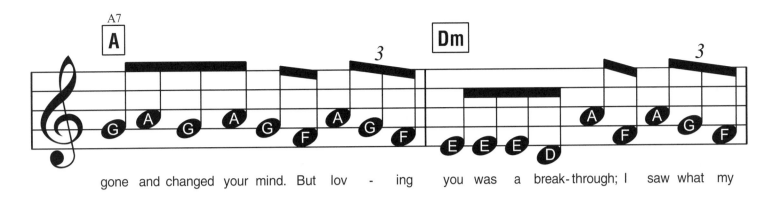

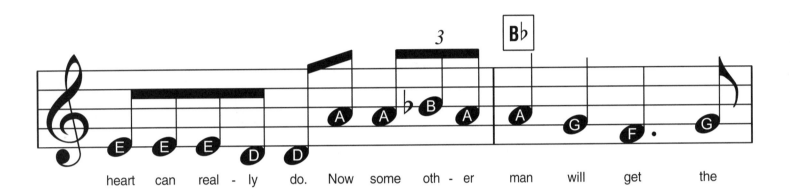

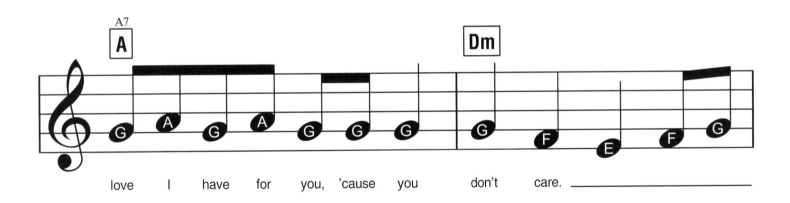

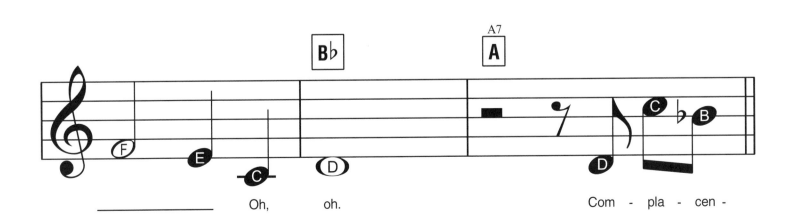

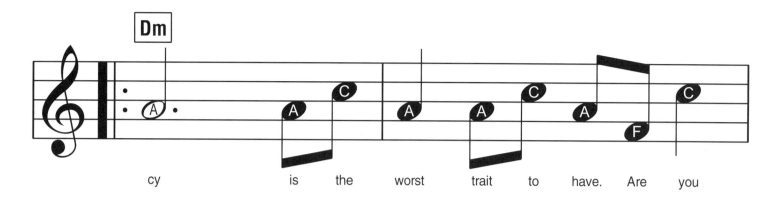

cy　　　　　is　the　worst　trait　to　have.　Are　you

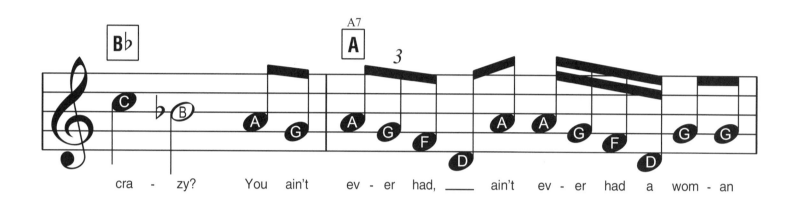

cra - zy?　You ain't　ev - er　had, ____ ain't　ev - er　had　a　wom - an

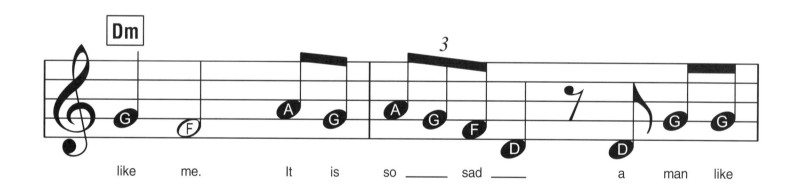

like　me.　It　is　so ____ sad ____　a　man　like

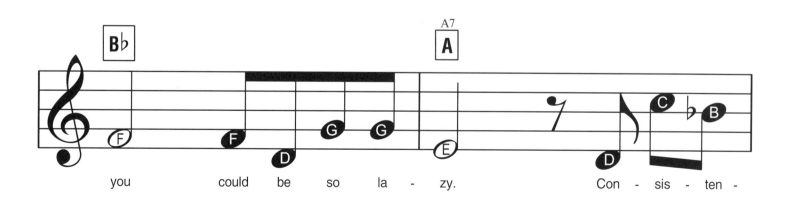

you　could　be　so　la - zy.　Con - sis - ten -

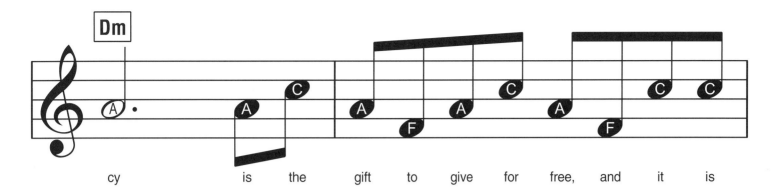

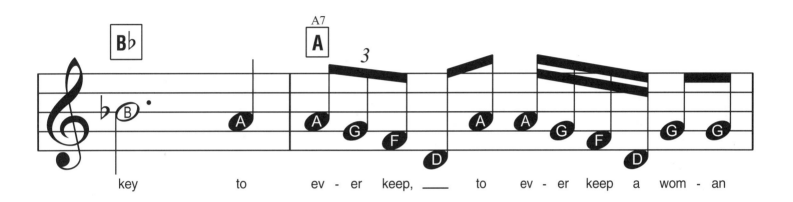

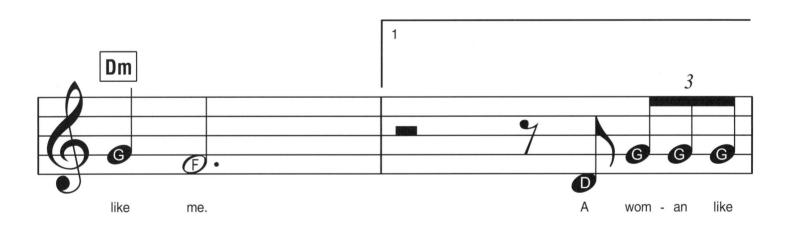

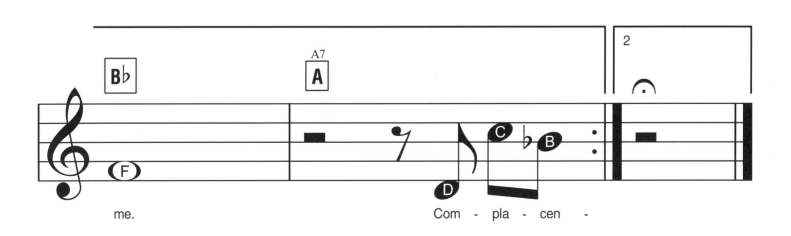

45

Hold On

Registration 8
Rhythm: Ballad or Gospel

Words and Music by Adele Adkins
and Dean Josiah Cover

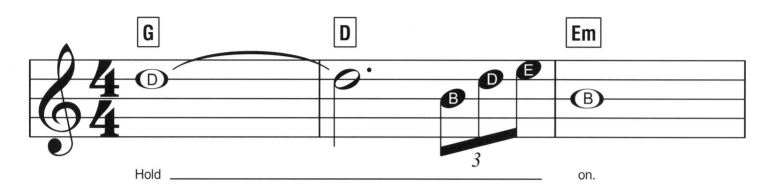

Hold _____ on.

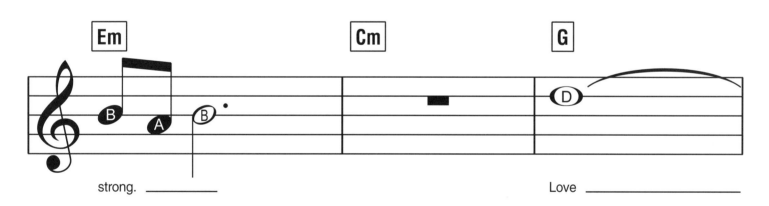

You _____ are still

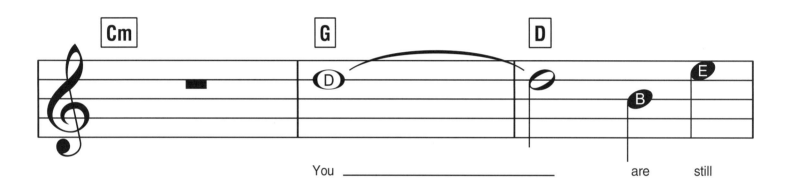

strong. _____ Love _____

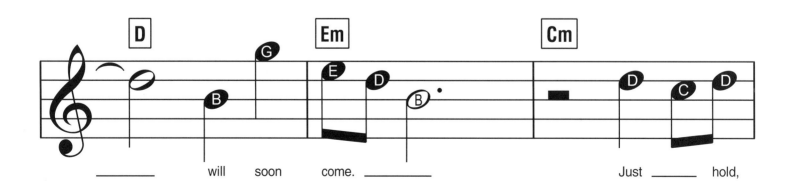

___ will soon come. _____ Just ____ hold,

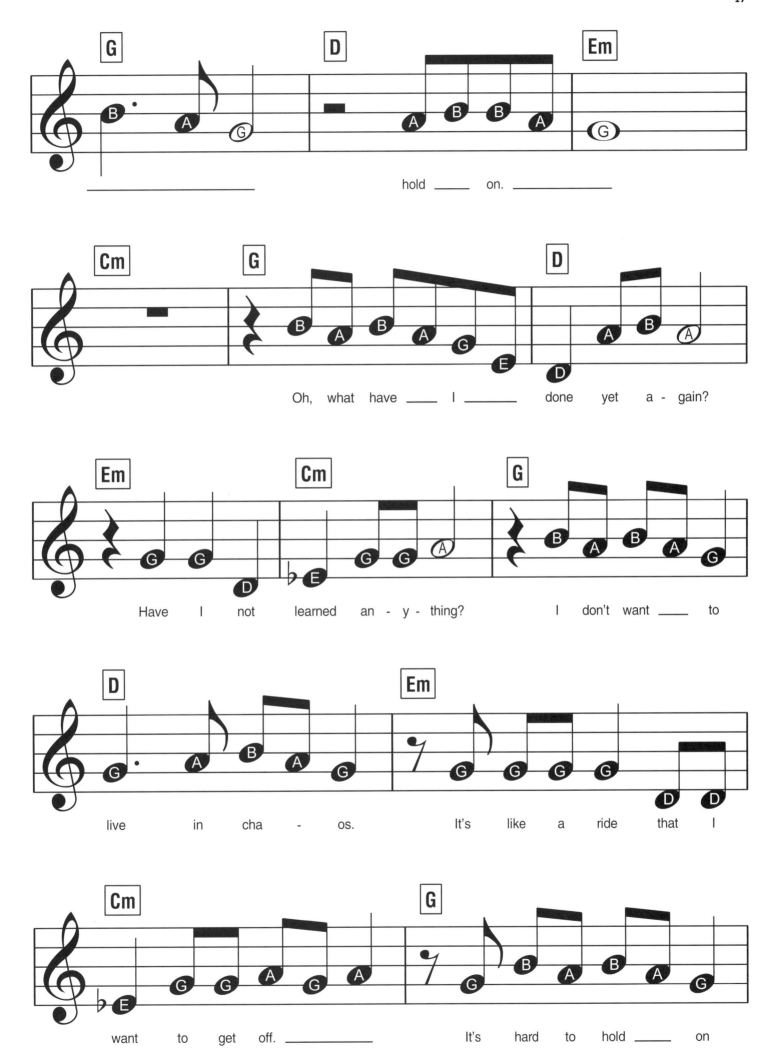

48

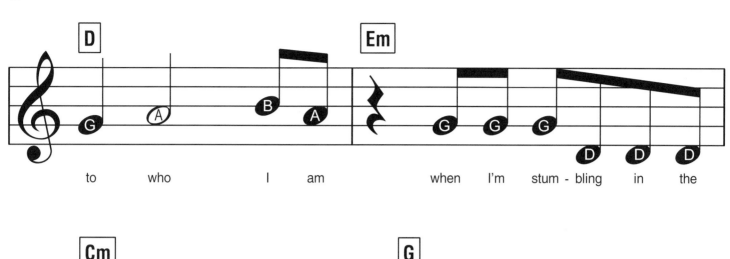

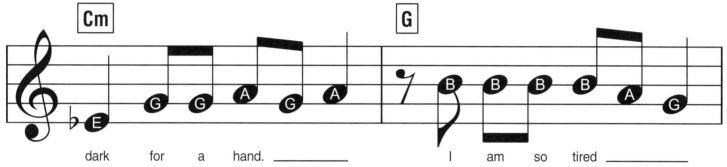

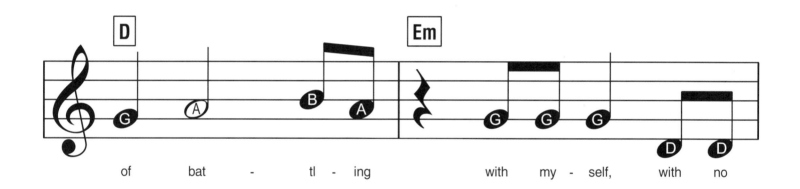

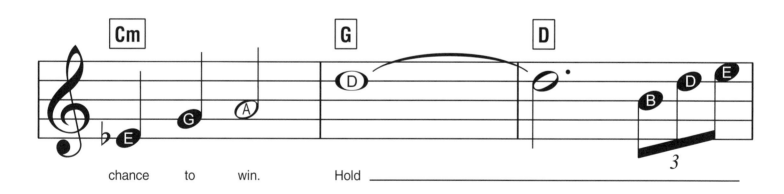

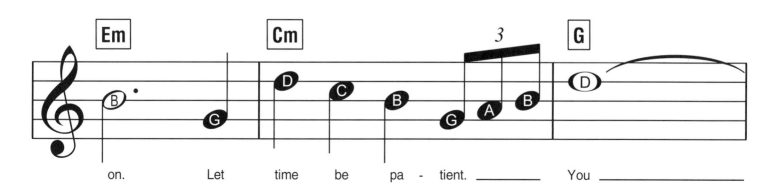

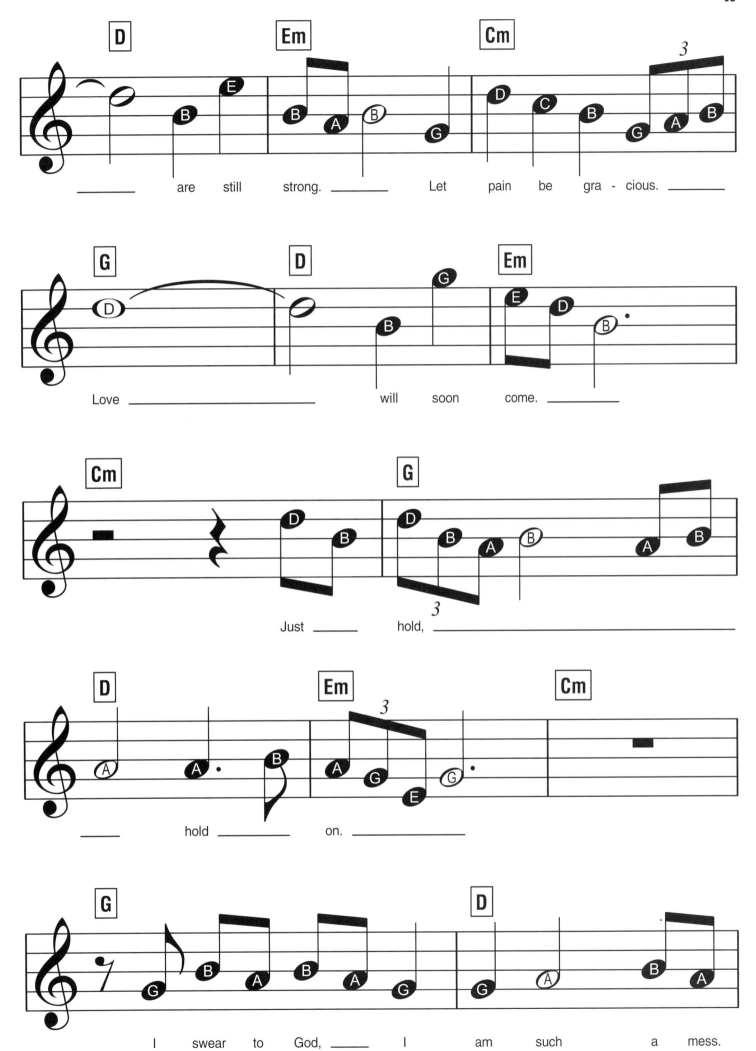

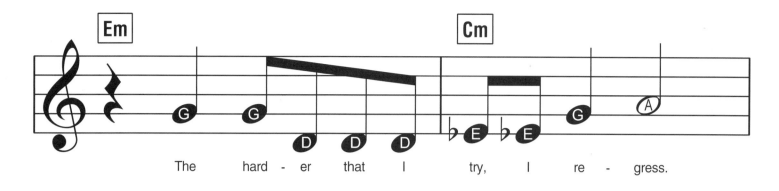

The hard - er that I try, I re - gress.

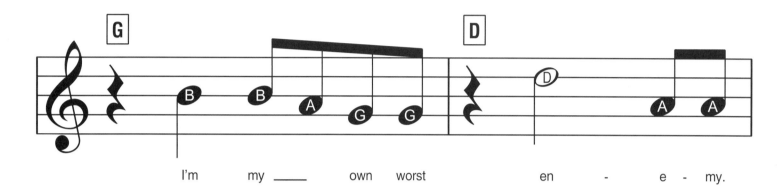

I'm my ____ own worst en - e - my.

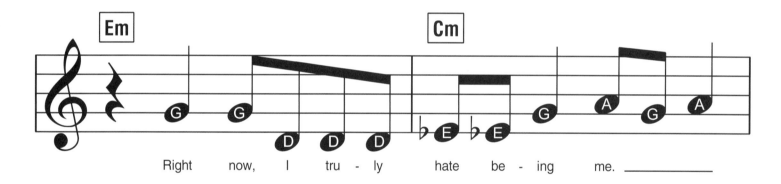

Right now, I tru - ly hate be - ing me. _____

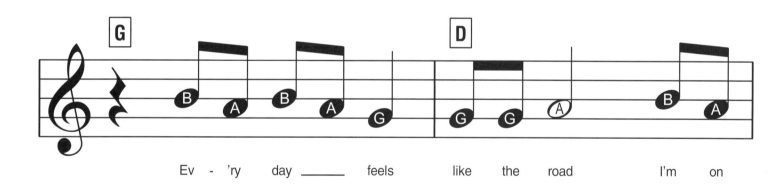

Ev - 'ry day ____ feels like the road I'm on

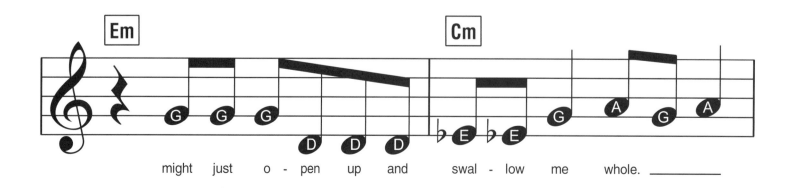

might just o - pen up and swal - low me whole. _____

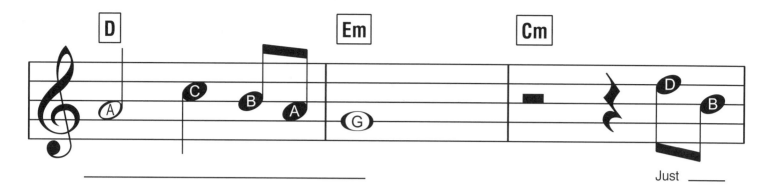

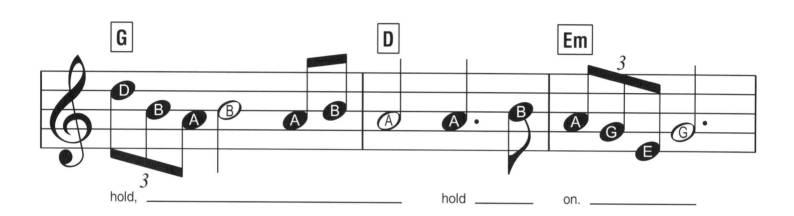

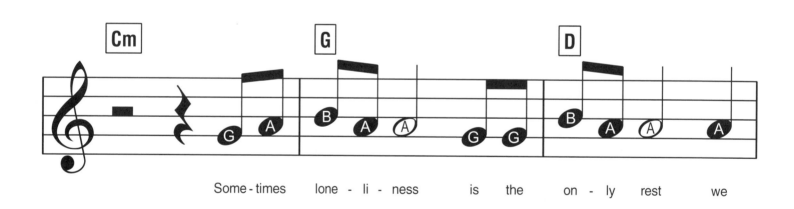

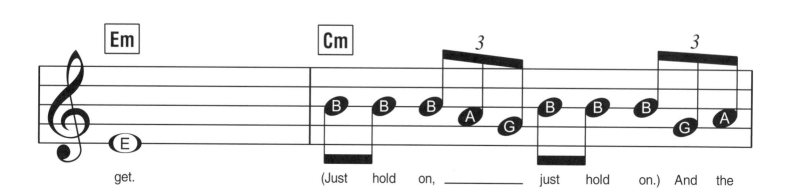

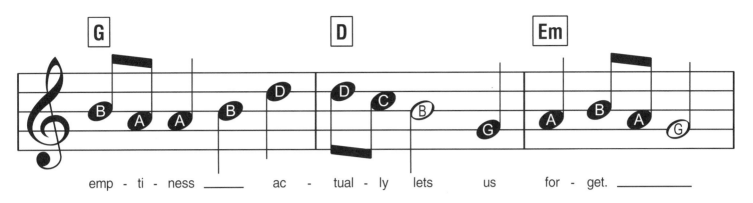

emp - ti - ness _____ ac - tual - ly lets us for - get. _____

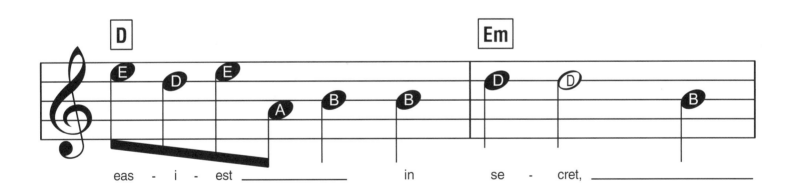

(Just hold on, _____ just hold on.) Some-times for - give - ness _____ is

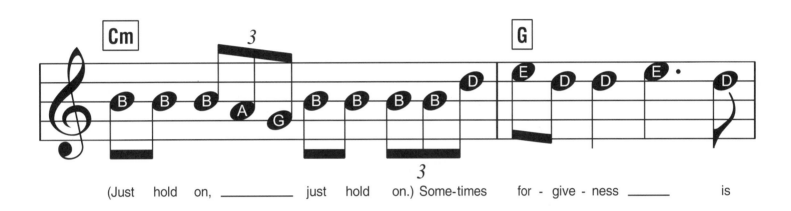

eas - i - est _____ in se - cret, _____

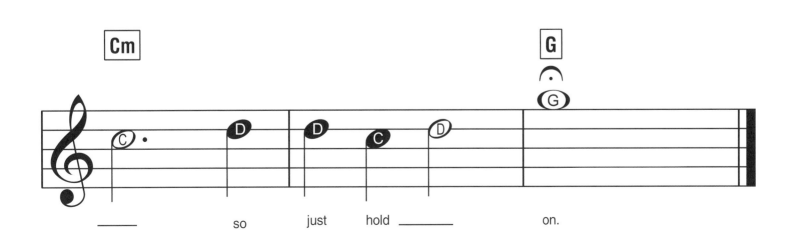

_____ so just hold _____ on.

Love Is a Game

Registration 3
Rhythm: Ballad

Words and Music by Adele Adkins
and Dean Josiah Cover

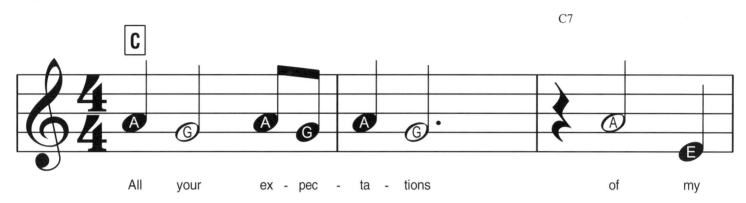

All your ex - pec - ta - tions of my

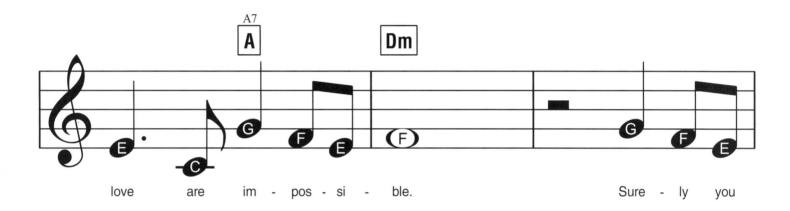

love are im - pos - si - ble. Sure - ly you

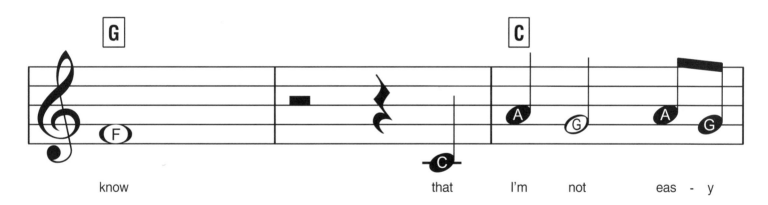

know that I'm not eas - y

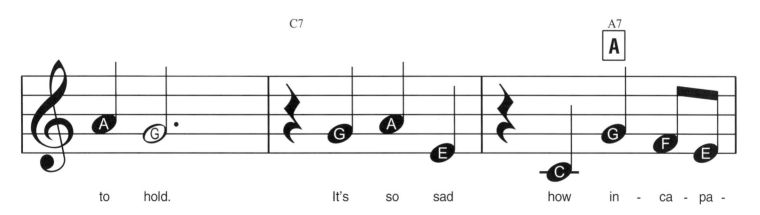

to hold. It's so sad how in - ca - pa -

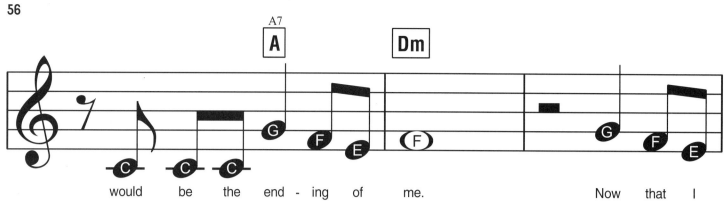

would be the end - ing of me. Now that I

Chorus

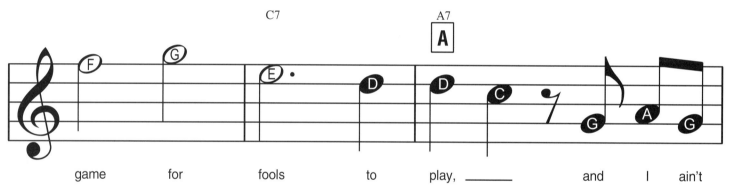

see _____ that (1., 2.) love
(3.) Love is a

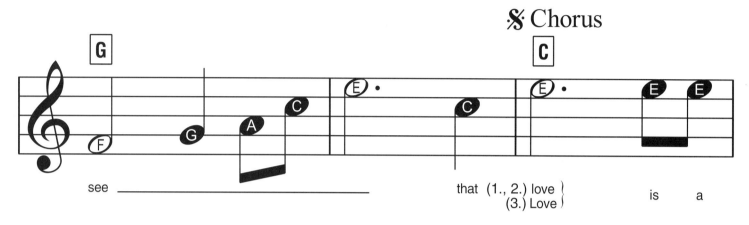

game for fools to play, _____ and I ain't

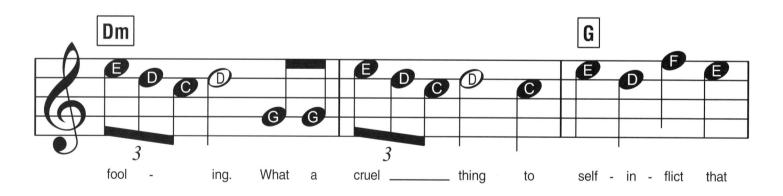

fool - ing. What a cruel _____ thing to self - in - flict that

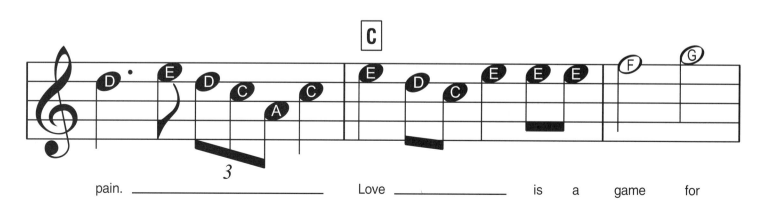

pain. _____ Love _____ is a game for

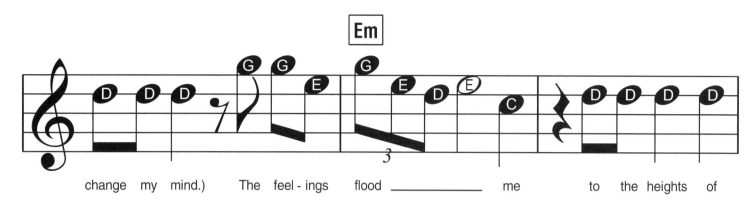

change my mind.) The feel - ings flood _____ me to the heights of

D.S. al Coda
(Return to 𝄋, play to ⊕
and skip to Coda)

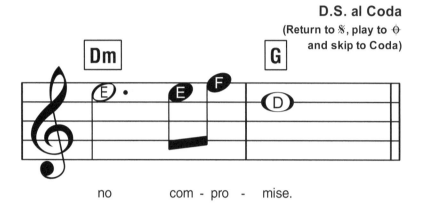

no com - pro - mise.

CODA

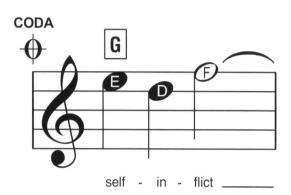

self - in - flict _____

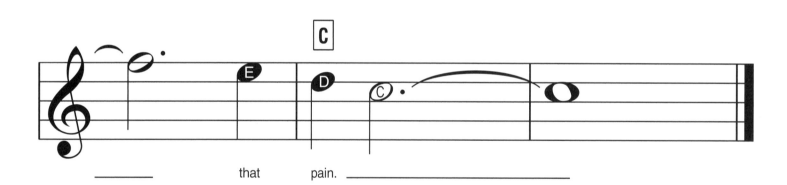

_____ that pain. _____

Additional Lyrics

2. How unbelievable of me to fall for the lies that I tell,
The dream that I sell,
When heartache, it's inevitable,
But I'm no good at doing it well.
Not that I care.
Why should anything about it be fair?
When... *(To Chorus)*

To Be Loved

Registration 8
Rhythm: Ballad

Words and Music by Adele Adkins
and Tobias Jesso Jr.

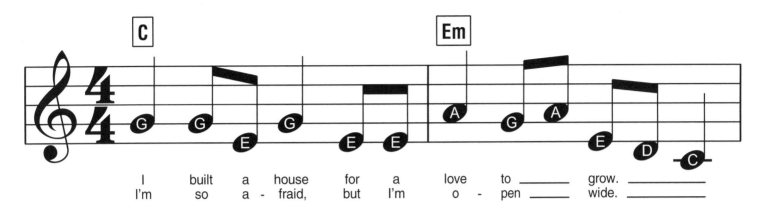

I built a house for a love to _____ grow. _____
I'm so a - fraid, but I'm o - pen _____ wide. _____

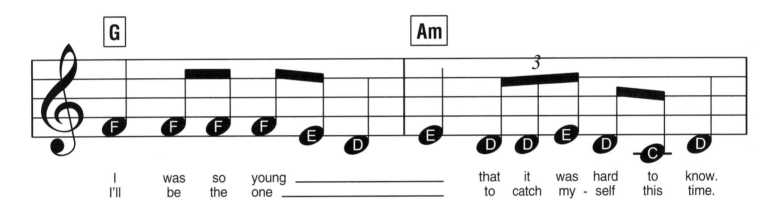

I was so young _____ that it was hard to know.
I'll be the one _____ to catch my - self this time.

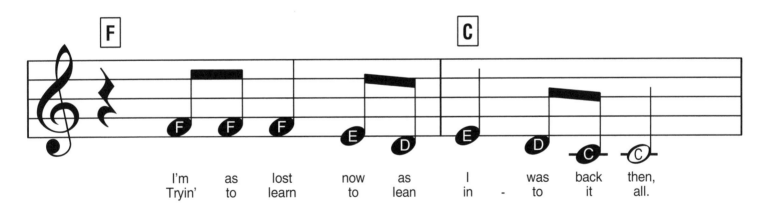

I'm as lost now as I was back then,
Tryin' to learn to lean in - to it all.

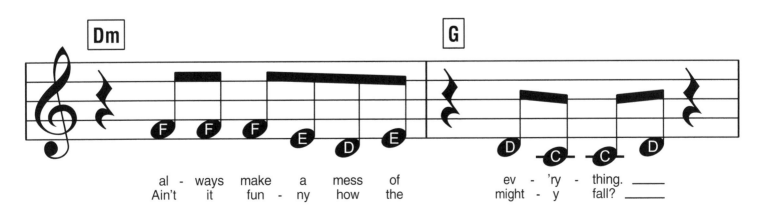

al - ways make a mess of ev - 'ry - thing. _____
Ain't it fun - ny how the might - y fall? _____

D.S. al Coda
(Return to 𝄋, play to ⊕
and skip to Coda)

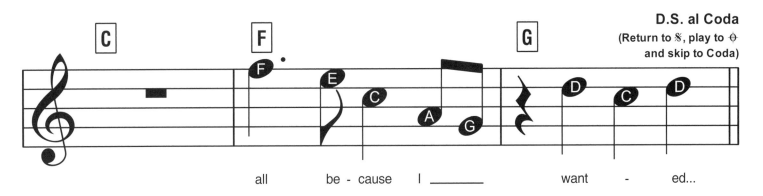

all be - cause I _____ want - ed...

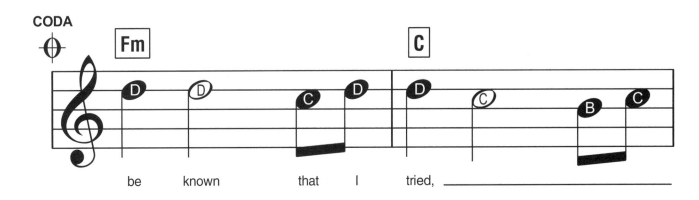

be known that I tried, _____

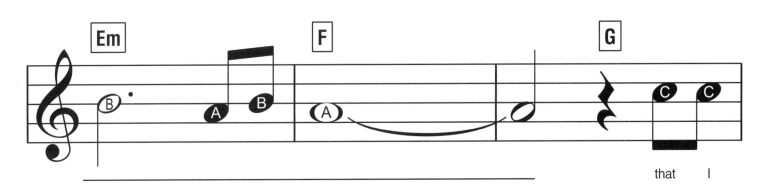

_____ that I

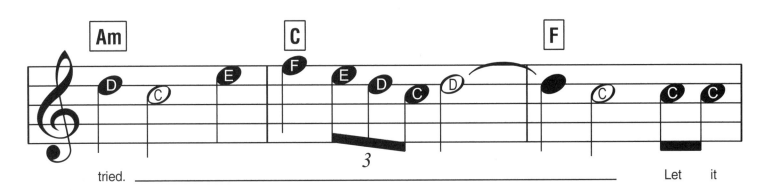

tried. _____ Let it

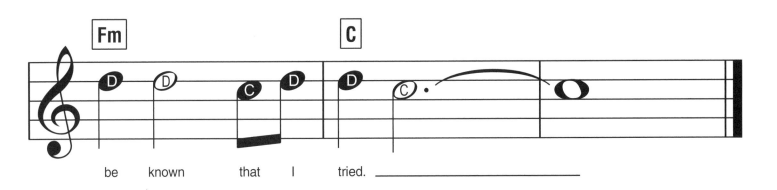

be known that I tried. _____

E-Z PLAY® TODAY SERIES

OVER 300 VOLUMES AVAILABLE!

The E-Z Play® Today songbook series is the shortest distance between beginning music and playing fun! Features of this series include:

- full-size books – large 9" x 12" format features easy-to-read, easy-to-play music

- accurate arrangements – simple enough for the beginner, but with authentic-sounding chords and melody lines

- minimum number of page turns

- thousands of songs – an incredible array of favorites, from classical and country to Christmas and contemporary hits

- lyrics – most arrangements include complete song lyrics

- most up-to-date registrations - books in the series contain a general registration guide, as well as individual song rhythm suggestions for today's electronic keyboards and organs

To see full descriptions of all the books in the series, visit:

HAL•LEONARD®

www.halleonard.com